100 WOMEN

WHO SHAPED WORLD HISTORY

GAIL MEYER ROLKA

sourcebooks
eXplore

Copyright © 1994, 2023 by Sourcebooks
Text by Gail Meyer Rolka
Cover design by Will Riley
Internal illustrations by AAARep/Sarah Gancho
Cover and internal design © 2023 by Sourcebooks

Sourcebooks and the colophon are registered trademarks of Sourcebooks.

Published by Sourcebooks eXplore, an imprint of Sourcebooks Kids
P.O. Box 4410, Naperville, Illinois 60567-4410
(630) 961-3900
sourcebookskids.com

Originally published in 1994 by Bluewood Books, an imprint of the Siyeh Group, Inc.

Cataloging-in-Publication Data is on file with the Library of Congress.

Source of Production: Versa Press, East Peoria, Illinois, USA
Date of Production: May 2023
Run Number: 5032108

Printed and bound in the United States of America.
VP 10 9 8 7 6 5 4 3 2 1

CONTENTS

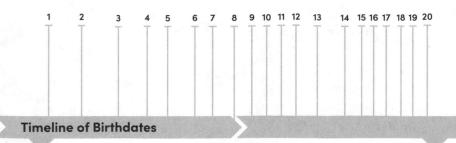

Timeline of Birthdates

1500 BCE   **1590 CE**

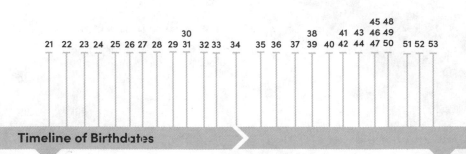

Timeline of Birthdates

1595   1835

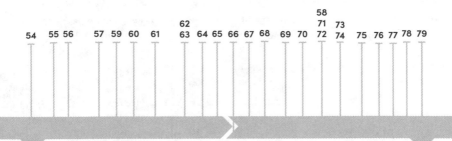

1840   1890

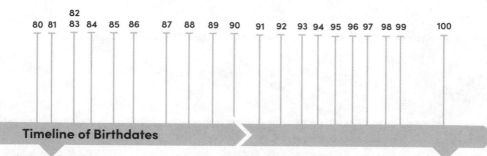

82
80 81 83 84 85 86 87 88 89 90 91 92 93 94 95 96 97 98 99 100

Timeline of Birthdates

1895 1960

INTRODUCTION

WHEN ANTHROPOLOGISTS discuss prehistoric humankind, they usually focus their attention on the role played by "man the hunter," while ignoring or de-emphasizing the more pivotal role of "woman the gatherer." Gathering—not hunting—was the primary survival activity of our ancestors, and this role was almost exclusively performed by women who developed the tools and technology needed to acquire, prepare, and preserve foods. First using simple implements such as sticks and flints for digging roots, women later invented the mortar and pestle and a rudimentary mill for grinding grains and seeds.

Around 10,000 BCE, the Agricultural Revolution, which is also known as the Neolithic Revolution, took place when humans progressed from being gatherers and hunters to farmers. This transition was facilitated by women gatherers who, over time, cultivated wild plants and developed new edible foods. In the Tigris and Euphrates valleys of Mesopotamia, women domesticated barley, flax, and wheat from wild grasses, whereas in China, they raised rice, and in North America, they grew potatoes and maize (corn). The heritage of these early women gatherers was kept alive by oral history.

After the invention of the wheel (c. 3500 BC), technology advanced dramatically. By 2400 BCE, the invention of devices such as the potter's wheel and metal tools transformed the manufacture of household goods and created a new class of specialized craftspeople and merchants. With planned agriculture, industry and trade flourished, and eventually societies developed written languages. However, once agriculture was undertaken on a large scale, women's role in food production was taken over by men. As humankind entered the era of written history, the accomplishments of men—and not those of women—were noted for posterity.

Until the late twentieth century, the recorded history of Western societies was overwhelmingly dominated by the exploits of men. With rare exceptions, information contained in traditional reference works, such as encyclopedias and history books, showed an undeniable bias toward the contributions of men while overlooking or downplaying those of women. For instance, though many women scientists were recognized and respected in their day, later historians tended to discredit their contributions. Also, because women often did not publish under their own names, historians failed entirely to recognize their efforts. Such was the case with **Marie Lavoisier**, whose twenty-five years of collaboration with her husband laid the groundwork for modern chemistry, and **Émilie du Châtelet**, a Newtonian scientist who greatly influenced the work of her companion, **Voltaire**. And what history text has given **Catherine Greene** credit for co-inventing the cotton gin with **Eli Whitney**?

Women, in fact, have not just kept the home fires burning and raised children for the past five thousand years. They have also advanced technology; discovered new lands; created innovative art, music, and dance; led armies; added to the body of important world literature; become influential national leaders; and questioned and changed existing social beliefs and structures to improve the quality of life for all people. To do so, many had to overcome formidable obstacles. Barred from entering university, mathematician **Sophie Germain** borrowed lecture notes, taught herself, and formulated a prize-winning theory. Without any formal education, **Madam C. J. Walker** started her own company and became the first self-made woman millionaire in America.

Many women made their mark in history by challenging society to provide equal rights for all citizens, often sacrificing their personal lives to reach this goal. **Dorothea Dix** and **Elizabeth Fry** crusaded for prison reform, and **Emmeline Pankhurst** and her daughters spearheaded the drive for women's suffrage in England. In America, **Susan B. Anthony** and **Carrie Chapman Catt**, among others, devoted their lives to securing voting rights for women. As Catt calculated, it took activists 51 years of continual effort—including 56 referenda to male voters, 480 submissions to state legislatures, 277 campaigns to obtain backing from state party conventions, 47 efforts to persuade state constitutional conventions, 30 campaigns to influence presidential parties, and 19 successive campaigns with 19 consecutive sessions of Congress—to achieve women's enfranchisement.

This book contains biographical sketches that celebrate the lives and achievements of 100 unique and talented women who lived in many parts of the globe from 1500 BC to the present. Some figures such as **Eleanor Roosevelt** and **Queen Victoria** are household names, but others, such as **Zenobia** and **Sophia Louisa Jex-Blake**, may not be as familiar. But all the women in this book have one thing in common: they helped shape the history of the world around them. Though the influence of some was primarily confined to their own lifetimes, the legacy of others, like that of **Queen Nzinga** of Ndondo and Matamba, or present-day Angola, survives today as an inspiration for a whole new generation.

◆ **HATSHEPSUT**, the sixth pharaoh of the Eighteenth Dynasty of Egypt, is not only remembered for her reign of peace and prosperity during which trade flourished but also for her glorious mortuary temple. Her temple—called the **Sublime of the Sublimes**—was built into the cliffs at Dayr al-Bahrī, opposite the temple of Karnak at Thebes. Its walls, inscribed with a pictorial account of the events of her life and their divine origins, are the source of most present-day knowledge about the female pharaoh.

Hatshepsut was the daughter of **Thutmose** I by his sister and major queen **Ahmose**. His successor, **Thutmose** II, his son by a lesser queen, followed Egyptian tradition and married his half sister Hatshepsut, who had only daughters. His heir, **Thutmose** III, was born of a union with a lesser wife named **Isis**. When Hatshepsut's husband died, she became the ruler for six-year-old Thutmose III, and in 1473 BCE she took the title of pharaoh for herself. Once on the throne, she announced that **Amon-Ra**, the king of the gods, had chosen her to rule. To further strengthen her position, she appointed the most eminent and talented men of her kingdom as advisors. One of these men was **Senenmut**, her chief of works and close confidante who became a "foster father" and tutor to her daughters. At Hatshepsut's direction, he restored the temple of the goddess Hathor at Cusae that had fallen into ruin. He also designed and built her a magnificent mortuary temple at Dayr al-Bahrī, which he placed on top of a series of three terraces, each flanked by porticoes that were supported by fluted columns. A double sphinx column led up to the lower terrace, where two four-sided stone pillars with pyramid-shaped tops were placed.

During her rule, Hatshepsut resumed trade with neighboring Negau, from which she obtained timber, and reopened the turquoise mines of Sinai. She also sent envoys south to negotiate trade agreements for metals and other commodities, such as panther skins and elephant tusks from coastal Libya. One of the most remarkable events in her reign was the expedition to Punt, which established a route down the Nile and over land to the Red Sea to obtain incense trees, whose grains were burned before statues of the pharaohs. Thirty-one of these trees were planted in front of the terraces at Dayr al-Bahrī.

When Thutmose III ascended the throne, he smashed the statues at Hatshepsut's beautiful temple and buried the pieces. Over 3,400 years later, archaeologists from the Metropolitan Museum of Art discovered many of the fragments and painstakingly restored them.

Known as **"a mother in Israel,"** a prophet, and a judge, **DEBORAH** is a biblical leader who rallied the tribes of Israel to defeat the Canaanite king **Jabin** and his military commander **Sisera** on the great plain of Jezreel by the Kishon River near Megiddo circa 1150 BCE. With the unifying element of religion, this victory welded together Israel's autonomous and scattered **tribes—Issachar, Zebulon,** and **Naphtali** from the north and Ephraim, Benjamin, and Manasseh from the south—and led to forty years of peace.

This story is vividly dramatized in the magnificent triumphal ode *Song of Deborah* in chapter five of the **book of Judges** in the Old Testament of the Bible.

Biblical "judges" were the freedom fighters of their era, renowned not only for their wise legal and religious judgments but also for their military leadership. When the people of Israel fell away from Yahweh—the Hebrew name of God used in the Bible—and were delivered into bondage or hardship, the scriptures state that a judge would be sent to lead them to victory and back to the practice of their religion.

Deborah, the only woman judge among many men, was the wife of **Lapidoth** and lived in the hill country of Ephraim between Bethel and Ramah. The Israelite tribes generally inhabited the mountainous highlands while the Canaanites—with their chariots, calvary, and strategic fortifications at Tannach, Megiddo, and Bethshan—controlled the plains and mountain passes through which caravan routes ran.

The narrative of Deborah states that she summoned **Barak** and instructed him to raise an army of ten thousand to meet Sisera in battle. Barak was unwilling to go unless she accompanied him, and she did, predicting that "the Lord will deliver Sisera into the hands of a woman" (Judg. 4:9). Despite Sisera's military advantage, the Israelites successfully routed their enemy, and Sisera fled on foot to the neighboring campsite of **Heber the Kenite**, who was friendly with King Jabin. Sisera sought refuge in Heber's tent and soon fell asleep, at which time Heber's wife **Jael** drove a tent peg into his head, thus fulfilling Deborah's prophecy (Judg. 4:21).

To commemorate this event, Deborah (or possibly a contemporary) composed the *Song of Deborah*. As the oldest surviving piece of biblical writing and the most elaborate of all early war songs, it is viewed by scholars as a masterpiece of Jewish poetry and is considered one of the finest odes in world literature. The ode, which Deborah sang following the victory at the annual festival when people offered gifts of thanksgiving to Yahweh, is also an account of great historical importance for our knowledge of the history of Israel. It is also unique for the fact that two women—Deborah and Jael—triumph as heroines.

3 SAPPHO (PSAPPHO)

c. 610–570 BCE

◆ Born in Mytilene on the Greek island of Lesbos, **SAPPHO** (or **PSAPPHO**, as she called herself) was so renowned as a poet that, two centuries after her death, **Plato** referred to her as "the tenth Muse." Although what is known about her life and work comes from fragments recorded by others, it appears that Sappho was one of four children born to a wealthy family, was married at an early age to a wealthy man named Cercylas, and had a daughter whom she named Cleis after her own mother. She was a contemporary of **Aesop**, King **Croesus**, and lyric poets **Stesichorus** and **Alcaeus**. She and Alcaeus were the first to write personal subjective prose, a form that is still popular today.

According to **Tullius Laurea**, Sappho wrote nine books of odes, wedding songs called epithalamiums, elegies, and hymns. However, there are few surviving fragments. The nine books appear to be arranged by meter. Book one, for instance, contains pieces written only in the **Sapphic stanza**, a form of verse she invented. These poems consist of four-line stanzas, in which the first three lines are each eleven syllables long and the fourth line is five syllables long.

While other poets glorified gods and heroes, Sappho's poems most commonly were about love, death, and passion. They were also filled with idyllic scenes from Greek life and the lives of women. Surviving fragments of her poetry include the *Ode of Aphrodite*, which was quoted by scholar **Dionysius of Halicarnassus** in the first century BCE. The work of many later Greek poets, including **Theocritus (c. 300–250 BCE)**, bear the mark of her influence.

Sappho taught music and poetry to a group of aristocratic young women, and when they would marry, she composed a special ode for the occasion. She also invented a twenty-one-string lyre that she used to accompany herself when she sang her poems. Sappho's writings were acclaimed for their beautiful diction, extreme simplicity of form, and great depth and intensity of emotion that made her poems unique. In contrast to other poets of her time, the language she used was not an artificially created literary dialect but rather ordinary speech, as shown in this poem about death:

We know this much
Death is an evil;
we have the gods'
word for it; they too
would die if death
were a good thing

Writing about **ASPASIA** over two thousand years after her death, American president **John Adams** said, "I wish some of our great men had such wives." Aspasia lived during one of the greatest ages in the history of the world, when classical civilizations flourished in ancient Greece and Rome. From this era, we can recall many famous men, such as philosophers **Socrates (c. 470–399 BCE)** and **Plato (c. 427–347 BCE)** and playwright **Euripides (c. 484–406 BCE)**. However, much less has been recorded about their female contemporaries because women were usually relegated to the roles of slaves, courtesans, or wives who were confined to the home and excluded from participation in public life.

Aspasia, who was born in Miletus in eastern Greece, arrived in Athens around 450 BC. Being a foreigner, she was not allowed to marry by law, so she became a *hetaira*, or highly educated female companions who, because they were unmarried, were free to study, attend lectures, and even engage in debates with men.

Known for her genius and great beauty, Aspasia opened a school of philosophy and rhetoric, and soon her home became the most popular salon in Athens. It was frequented by leading scholars, politicians, and artists, including Plato and Socrates, to whom she is credited as teaching the art of eloquence. Also in attendance was **Pericles (c. 495–429 BCE)**, a chief Athenian strategos. His thirty-year administration, later known as the **Age of Pericles**, was a time when Athens became a democratic state and reigned as the intellectual and artistic center of the country.

Pericles fell in love with Aspasia, but she was not of Athenian birth and therefore could not legally become his wife. Since he had divorced his wife, Aspasia became his consort. From then on, Aspasia acted as his political advisor and confidante, supporting him in his struggle against the aristocracy to establish a democracy. Some historians hold her responsible for the disastrous **Peloponnesian War (431–421 BC)**, which they believe Pericles waged at her urging. Others claim that she wrote the eloquent Funeral Oration, which Pericles delivered to his troops at the conclusion of the war.

After the deaths of his two legitimate sons by his wife, Pericles enacted a law to make Pericles, his son by Aspasia, an Athenian citizen. Young Pericles later became an army general. Unable to criticize Pericles directly, Athenians who were angry over his relationship with Aspasia charged her with impiety, or acting disrespectful toward the gods. After an impassioned, tearful defense by Pericles, she was found innocent.

◆ A beautiful and politically ambitious woman, **CLEOPATRA VII** was the daughter of **Ptolemy XII Auletes (c. 117–51 BCE)**, Macedonian king of Egypt. Her father died when she was eighteen, and by custom, she was wed to her younger brother, **Ptolemy XIII (62–47 BCE)**. They began a joint rule in 51 BCE but Ptolemy, prompted by advisors, seized total control and drove his sister into exile. In 48 BCE in Alexandria, she met Roman General **Gaius Julius Caesar (100–44 BCE)**, who became enamored of her. He undertook a war on her behalf against her brother, in which Ptolemy was killed, and he then declared Cleopatra the queen of Egypt.

Following her required marriage to her next younger brother, **Ptolemy XIV (59–44 BCE)**, Cleopatra gave birth to a son, **Caesarion (47–30 BCE)**, who she claimed to be Caesar's son. On several occasions, Cleopatra visited Caesar in Rome, where he had a gold statue built in her honor and provided her with a luxurious villa near the Tiber River. When Caesar was assassinated in 44 BCE, Cleopatra ascended the throne, after likely poisoning her husband-brother, and installed her young son as her co-ruler.

Shortly after this, **Marcus Antonius a.k.a. Mark Antony (83–30 BCE),** commander of the eastern provinces of the Roman Empire, summoned Cleopatra to Rome for a meeting. He fell in love with her and spent a season with her, during which time they had two daughters. Antony was recalled to Rome to marry Octavia, sister of Caesar's great-nephew and heir **Octavian (63 BCE–14 CE)**. But in 36 BCE, **Antony** returned to the east as commander of an expedition against the Parthians, at which time he reunited with Cleopatra at Antioch. Beyond their legendary love affair, the union of Antony and Cleopatra was a political act that united all of Rome against Antony. Angry at Antony's affair and fearful that he and Cleopatra planned to take control of the eastern half of the Roman Empire, Octavian declared war against them in 32 BCE.

At the **Battle of Actium** in 31 BCE, Cleopatra withdrew her naval fleet, believing that defeat was inevitable, and she and Antony fled to Alexandria. Receiving a false report that Cleopatra had already committed suicide, Antony killed himself. When Cleopatra learned Octavian planned to exhibit her in Rome as proof of his triumph, she committed suicide by taking poison, although another traditional story says she died from the bite of an asp.

As a result, Octavian killed Cleopatra's son Caesarion, who was the last of the Ptolemaic dynasty, and turned Egypt into a Roman province. Octavian then became the first sole ruler of the Roman Empire and reigned until his death in 14 CE.

◆ All historical knowledge about the life of **MARY** is contained in the **Gospels** written by the apostles **Matthew, Mark, Luke,** and **John,** which are part of the New Testament of the Bible. According to Christian belief, **Jesus Christ**—the son of God born on earth in human form—was the Messiah who had come to free the people of Israel from the bonds of Roman rule and lead them to a new kingdom. As Jesus' mother, Mary occupies an important role in theology and worship to the over 2.3 billion Christians in the world, particularly to those belonging to the Catholic Church.

Historians estimate that Mary was between sixteen and eighteen years old at the time of her son's birth around 4 BCE. However, the precise circumstances of her death are unknown, and the Gospels provide only brief glimpses into her life. She belonged to the house of David, lived in lower Galilee (Luke 1:26), and became engaged to a carpenter named Joseph (Matthew 1:18).

The angel Gabriel told her that, though

she was a virgin, she would conceive the son of God (Luke 1:26). Beginning in Luke 1:46, Mary visited her cousin Elizabeth and recited the Magnificat ("My soul glorifies the Lord..."). She was a silent presence at her son's birth and the visits of the shepherds and Magi (Matthew 2:1) and when Jesus was presented at the temple (Luke 2:22). Later, when she finds him teaching at the temple, she utters the second of only three recorded statements: "Son, why have you treated us like this? Your father and I have been anxiously searching for you." (Luke 2:48). Her last recorded statement was at the marriage feast at Cana when she told Jesus "They have no wine," prompting him to perform his first miracle of changing water into wine (John 2:3). She is last seen at the foot of the cross weeping when Jesus dies (John 19:25).

Known from scriptures as the **Virgin Mary,** Christians soon began to honor Mary as the **Mother of God—Theotokos.** By the seventh century, they came to believe she had remained a virgin all her life, or **"ever virgin."** In the Middle Ages, Mary's perpetual purity came to imply that she was free from all sin, including original sin, later defined in Roman Catholic dogma as the **Immaculate Conception** (1854). In 1950, Pope Pius XII decreed that Mary, at the end of her earthly life, had been assumed, body and soul, into heaven.

Mary's reported appearances over many years to fervent believers on Earth led to many shrines built in her honor around the world. The most famous of these are the **Black Madonna of Częstochowa** in Poland, revered since the fourteenth century; the picture of **Our Lady of Guadalupe** commemorating an appearance in Mexico in 1531; **Our Lady of Lourdes** in France in 1858; and **Our Lady of Fátima** in Portugal in 1917.

◆ **BOADICEA** became queen of the **Iceni** tribe in 60 AD upon the death of her husband, **King Prasutagus**, who had ruled what is now Norfolk and Sussex counties in England as a client king under the jurisdiction of the Roman **Emperor Nero (37–68 AD)**. Prasutagus tried to ensure imperial protection for his family by leaving a will that divided his lands equally between his two daughters and Nero. However, after his death, Nero immediately annexed all of his lands, and his soldiers tortured Boadicea, assaulted her daughters, and enslaved the Iceni tribesmen.

Enraged, the proud queen called her people together to expel the Roman invaders, amassing a native force of over one hundred thousand strong, including Celtic women and children. For many years, Roman taxation in East Anglia had been extremely burdensome, and the cruel suppression of the Iceni was the catalyst for action. With the Roman **Governor General Suetonius Paulinus** and his troops away fighting Druids in North Wales, the situation was favorable for a full revolt.

Boadicea's forces destroyed the Roman colony at Camulodunum (now Colchester), sacked Londinium (now London), burned the tribal capital of Veralamium (now St. Albans), and leveled several military outposts. According to historian **Cornelius Tacitus (c. 56–120 AD)**, Boadicea's forces killed some seventy thousand Roman soldiers and British sympathizers, and they nearly annihilated the Ninth Roman Legion that had been marching from Lincoln as reinforcement.

Returning with ten thousand soldiers, Suetonius met the Celts in the field near Fenny Stratford. Boadicea herself rode into battle, accompanied by her two daughters. Several days of fierce combat turned into one of the worst slaughters in British history, with eighty thousand killed by the Romans, equaling nearly one-tenth of all Celts in England. To prevent being captured, Boadicea took poison and died.

As a result of Boadicea's revolt, the Roman government adopted a fairer policy of governing Britain, and Suetonius was replaced by a more reasonable governor. Nero, who had levied huge taxes to rebuild Rome and indulged in murderous excesses toward suspected enemies, was condemned to die by the Roman Senate. Prior to being executed, he committed suicide.

In 1902, a memorial statue of Boadicea, clutching a spear as she commands a chariot pulled by two rearing horses, was erected near the Westminster Bridge over the Thames river, facing Parliament in London. Inscribed on its base are the words: "Regions Caesar never knew/ Thy Posterity shall sway."

◆ A brilliant and ambitious woman, **ZENOBIA**, or **Znwbyā Bat Zabbai** in Aramaic, was the daughter of a wealthy Arab merchant and was born in the desert city of Palmyra in present-day Syria. Her military quest to make Palmyra supreme in the eastern region of the Roman Empire made her a heroine of her time.

The opulent city of Palmyra lay at the crossroads of vital caravan routes between Rome and Persia. Zenobia's husband, **Septimius Odaenathus (c. 220–266 CE)**, ruled it as a client king of Rome. After Roman **Emperor Valerian** was murdered by **King Shāpūr I** of Persia in 260 CE, Odaenathus, hoping to increase his stature with Rome, crushed Persia. Zenobia, who often hunted panther and other game with her husband and disdained a chariot in favor of a horse, accompanied him. After his death in 266 CE, she decided to extend his conquests to make Palmyra the undisputed power in the region.

Rather than ruling on behalf of her son **Wahballat**, Zenobia ascended the throne and declared herself queen of the east. She immediately attacked Egypt while the armies of Rome were fighting a barbarian invasion of Italy, and by 269 CE, most of Egypt fell to her general **Zabdas**. She then annexed the majority of Syria, and by 270 CE, she had extended her domain into Asia Minor as far as Bithynia on the Bosporus Strait. She now not only controlled vital commerce to Rome, but also the trade routes with Abyssinia, Arabia, and India.

Declaring herself independent of Rome, Zenobia ruled an empire that was founded on tolerance rather than persecution. She established cordial relations with Jews at Alexandria as well as with **Paul of Samosata**. During the brief time that her court flourished, it became known for its intellectual distinction as well as its extravagant show of wealth.

When **Emperor Aurelian (215–275 CE)** came to power in 270 CE, he recognized the threat that Zenobia posed to the unity of the Roman Empire. Within a year, he reclaimed Egypt and Asia Minor and lay siege to Palmyra itself. Zenobia and her son escaped the city only to be captured while boarding a boat in Euphrates on their way to seek support from Persia. After parading her through the streets of Rome bedecked in jewels as a symbol of his conquest, Aurelian set her free. She later married a Roman senator and retired in affluent luxury to a villa in Tibur (now Tivoli), where she opened a fashionable salon.

Shortly before his death in 275 CE, Aurelian was compelled to return to Palmyra to quell another insurrection. This time the city was plundered, and its civilization disappeared in the desert sands.

Although it is **Constantine the Great (c. 272–337 CE)** who is given credit for establishing **Christianity** as the dominant religion of the Western world, it was the influence and good works of his mother **HELENA** that served to greatly expedite the spread of the faith. Some historians even contend that Helena became a Christian before her son and was responsible for his conversion. Others, citing the number of churches she founded, consider her to be the **Mother of Christianity**.

Helena was born in Drepanum in the ancient Roman province of Bithynia on the Nicomedian Gulf. The daughter of an innkeeper, she met **Constantius (d. 306 AD)** when he passed through her district while engaged in a military conquest. After nineteen years together, during which time she gave birth to her only son named Constantine, Constantius abandoned her when he became ruler of the **Roman Empire** so he could marry the stepdaughter of his patron, **Emperor Maximianus Herculius**.

After his father died in 306 CE, Constantine succeeded as emperor and summoned Helena to his court in Rome. He conferred on her the title of Augusta, dowager empress. To further honor his mother, he renamed her birthplace **Helenopolis** and had her image imprinted on coins.

Helena, who was very religious and devout, made a pilgrimage to the Holy Land and visited Jerusalem in 324 CE. Excavating beneath the rubble of a pagan temple, she found pieces of wood that she claimed were remnants of the true cross on which Jesus Christ had been crucified three centuries prior. On this site, she founded the **Church of the Holy Sepulchre**. She then traveled to Bethlehem to locate the birthplace of Jesus and built the **Church of the Nativity** on what she believed to be the site. Although these sites have never been historically authenticated and are at best educated guesses on Helena's part, the churches still draw thousands of pilgrims annually.

After founding many more churches, Helena rejoined her son, who had moved his capital from Rome to Constantinople, and she died there at the age of eighty. Immediately upon her death, she was revered as a saint. Constantine had her buried in the imperial vault of the Church of the Apostles, but around 849 CE, her body was transferred to the **Hautvillers Abbey** near Rheims, France, where her resting place continues to be a place of pilgrimage. In the Roman Catholic Church, her feast day is celebrated as August 18. In the Eastern Orthodox Church, her feast day is celebrated jointly with that of her son on May 21.

Known as the first woman mathematician, **HYPATIA** was also a philosopher, scientist, and scholar. Born in Alexandria, she was raised by her father **Theon** after her mother died when she was a baby. A university mathematics professor and noted astronomer, he supervised every aspect of Hypatia's education. Under his tutelage, she studied mathematics, science, literature, philosophy, and the arts, while also engaging in a vigorous daily routine of exercise with him.

After attending a school in Athens taught by **Plutarch (46–119 CE)**, Hypatia returned to Alexandria and became a professor at the university, where she is said to have occupied the chair of platonic philosophy. Hypatia was considered something of an oracle, and students from many areas of the country were drawn to Alexandria to hear her inspired lectures on mathematics and to study with her.

Most of what we know about Hypatia today comes from letters she wrote to one of her pupils, **Synesius of Cyrene** in Greece, who later became bishop of Ptolemais in 411 CE. Hypatia suggested that Synesius measure the positions of stars and planets with an **astrolabe** and a **planisphere**, astronomical instruments that she had designed.

Hypatia retained her Greek religious traditions even though Christianity was becoming dominant in Alexandria. She is believed to have become a victim of a power struggle between her friend **Orestes**, the Roman governor of Egypt, and **Cyril**, the Christian patriarch of Alexandria who was committed to eliminating what he viewed as heretical religious beliefs. Inflamed by Cyril, a mob kidnapped and murdered Hypatia in 415 CE.

Some historians view Hypatia's death as marking the end of the golden age of Greek mathematics. Hundreds of years later, it is still unclear how the two libraries in Alexandria were destroyed. Regardless, these tragic events ended a millennium of sophisticated academics.

As described by Byzantine historian **Procopius (c. 500–565 CE)** in his book *Secret History (Anecdota)*, **THEODORA** was the daughter of **Acacius**, the bear keeper at the Hippodrome in Constantinople (now Istanbul). Orphaned at the age of four, she joined her sister in the theater. By age fifteen, she was a well-known dancer and mime, who was renowned for her beauty and comedic talents. On her travels through Egypt, she encountered **Timothy Aelurus, a Monophysite Patriarch** (one who believed that Jesus Christ had a composite nature that was both human and divine) who greatly influenced her religious education.

While working as a wool spinner in Constantinople, Theodora met **Justinian I (483–565 CE)**, heir to the Byzantine throne, who was twenty years her senior, and he fell in love with her. In 523 CE, his uncle, **Justin I (450–527 CE)**, repealed the law which forbade the marriage of senators and women of the stage, and they were wed.

Upon his uncle's death, Justinian ascended the throne and made Theodora his co-ruler. Her skill and authority immediately became evident in all facets of administrative, religious, and political affairs. Early on in their joint reign, an insurrection known as the **Nika riots (532 CE)** broke out in Constantinople as a result of high taxes and other political conflicts. Theodora convinced her husband not to flee the city when the rebels arrives, which allowed his troops, commanded by **General Belisarius**, to disperse the rioters.

Although totally committed to her husband's vision of rebuilding the Roman Empire, Theodora remained opposed to expanding their holdings through continual warfare. History has shown her view to be the wiser choice. Justinian is best known for his codification of Roman law, a process which took a whole decade, and Theodora exerted a great deal of influence on his thinking. The result of his work, the *Codex* and other volumes, still form the basis of the legal systems in many European countries.

Theodora's devotion to social justice for women was unique for her time. During her reign, divorce laws were modified, daughters could inherit, wives were allowed to retain their dowries as their own property, and children could not be sold as slaves to pay off their parents' debts. An edict in the year 535 CE outlawed brothels in the major cities, and Theodora, at her own expense, purchased the freedom of five hundred girls who had been sold into prostitution and provided a house for them near the Black Sea. After she died of cancer at the age of fifty-one, Justinian was so distraught that little effective legislation passed during the final seventeen years of his life.

As queen of France (1137–1152), queen of England (1154–1204), and the mother of two English kings, **Richard I (1157–1199,** called **Richard the Lion Hearted)** and John I **(1167–1216), ELEANOR OF AQUITAINE** was one of the most politically influential women of her time. Born in France, the daughter of **William X** of Aquitaine, she was wed to **King Louis VII** of France in 1137. During fifteen years of marriage, she bore two daughters and accompanied her husband on the **Second Crusade** to the Holy Land between 1147 and 1149, taking with her three hundred women both to fight and to nurse the wounded. By mutual consent, their marriage was annulled in 1152.

Besieged by suitors, Eleanor married Henry Plantagenet, count of Anjou, who in 1154 became **King Henry II (1133–1189),** the first Plantagenet king of England, and she subsequently bore him five sons and three daughters. She brought to the marriage the extensive Duchy of Aquitaine, Gascony, and Poitiers, which she had inherited from her father at age fifteen. This event marked the beginning of the conflict between France and England that persisted through the **Middle Ages**. In 1170, she convinced Henry to invest in their son Richard with the lands.

Henry's continued unfaithfulness alienated Eleanor, so when her sons Richard and John rebelled against their father in 1173, she sided with them. After they were unsuccessful in their attempt to overthrow their father, she was captured while attempting to flee and imprisoned until her husband's death in 1189. Once released, she became a powerful presence at court, granting amnesty to prisoners and securing the succession of her son Richard to the throne. She ruled on his behalf during his absence during the **Third Crusade**, thwarting an attempt by John to conspire with France against England. Upon

Richard's return in 1194, she negotiated a reconciliation between the two brothers, which served to maintain peace in England and ensure John's succession to the throne

Eleanor's influence also extend J to culture and education. In both England and France, where she reigned as queen for a total of sixty-five years, she gathered leading poets, scholars, and musicians at her courts and founded educational institutions. In her eighties, she arranged the marriage of her granddaughter **Blanche of Castile** to **King Louis VIII** of France and successfully defended her French territories against assaults. Through the marriages of her daughters, she created alliances with several ruling houses in Europe. She retired to the Fontevrault Abbey in France, where she died at the age of eighty-two in 1201.

◆ Beloved by the people of her country, **TAMARA (TAMAR)**, the great medieval queen of Georgia, brought her kingdom to the peak of its glory before Mongol **Genghis Khan (c. 1158- 1227)** destroyed its capital of Tiflis (now Tbilisi) in 1236. The memory of the golden age she helped create lives on today in Georgian myths and history.

The feudal kingdom of Georgia was located in a pivotal position on the cross-roads between Europe, China, and the Middle East. It was bounded on the west by the Black Sea; on the east by the Caspian Sea, across which lay Persia, India, and Central Asia; on the north by the Caucasus Mountains, a barricade against Russia; and on the south by Armenia's mountainous plateau, a buffer against the Turkish Empire. Georgia was converted to Christianity in the fourth century, and in the eighth century, the House of Bagrationi first gained the throne, later reaching its height under Tamara's great-grandfather, **King David IV** (known as **David the Builder, 1073–1125)**.

Six years before his death, Tamara's father, **King Giorgi III (d. 1184)**, crowned her as his co-ruler in 1178, giving her the title of "Mountain of God." To fulfill her duty to produce an heir, she married **Yury Bogolyubsky** from southern Russia in 1187. They were an ill-matched pair and produced no children, so Tamara—in stark contrast to her father's grisly disposal of unwanted relatives—sent Giorgi into exile. For the next twenty years, Giorgi continued to lead revolts to overthrow her, but each time his efforts failed, Tamara merely sent him back into exile. After her marriage to **David Sosland**, a prince of the Bagrationi line, produced two children, she pursued her goal of restoring Georgia to its former might.

From the year 1200 until her death, Tamara undertook one successful military campaign after another, including a victory at the famous Battle of Basiani (1205), where the Turkish sultan surrendered Kars, over which she appointed her son Giorgi governor. After Byzantium was returned to Christianity by the **Fourth Crusade** in 1204, she turned it into a protectorate. She also established numerous other Muslim protectorates and extended her kingdom north beyond the Caucasus Mountains.

Under Tamara's guidance, Georgia experienced a great renaissance of arts and letters, which inspired national poet **Shota Rustaveli** to write his famous 1,600-quatrain epic poem *The Knight in Panther's Skin.* Dedicated to Tamara, it symbolically describes Georgia's glorious era under her rule, calling her "radiant as the rising sun, born to illuminate the world around her... Woman though she is, God had created her to be a sovereign. We may say without flattery that she knows how to rule..."

In 1397, **MARGARET I** succeeded in uniting the Scandinavian kingdoms of Denmark, Norway, and Sweden, a unique accomplishment in the history of the three countries, and the tripartite union she forged endured for 136 years. A descendant of **Canute (c. 994–1035)**, the first Danish king of England, and the daughter of **King Valdemar IV**, she was married at age ten to **Haakon VI of Norway (1340–1380)**, the son of **Magnus Eriksson** of Sweden and Norway. Although Haakon lost the Swedish crown a year later, he remained sovereign over Norway, and Margaret, an accomplished scholar, grew up in the Norwegian court.

Margaret's son **Olaf V** was born in 1370. Upon Margaret's father Voldemar's death in 1375, the Danes accepted Olaf as their king, and when Haakon died in 1380, the crown of Norway also passed to Olaf, with Margaret ruling on his behalf. In 1387, Olaf died, and she was declared "sovereign lady and ruler" of both countries. To provide a male ruler, she adopted her grandnephew **Eric of Pomerania (Eric III) (c. 1381–1459)** in 1389. She then turned her attention to Sweden, where angry nobles had rebelled against their German **King Albert of Mecklenburg**. After defeating Albert's army, she imprisoned him.

The **Hanseatic League** intervened and ordered Albert released on the condition he pay Margaret 60,000 Marks. When he failed to do so, Margaret gained control of Sweden. In June 1397, the three countries were united for the first and only time in history under Margaret's control when Eric was crowned king. Even after Eric came of age in 1401, Margaret continued to rule for him. In a commanding but diplomatic way, she moved to consolidate her power and centralize her authority. She did this by setting up a network of provincial sheriffs who governed their own native territories, a system that served to strengthen allegiance to the crown rather than to a region. She also reformed Danish currency and built up the royal treasury through taxation and by reclamation of hundreds of estates in Denmark and Sweden that had once belonged to the crown.

In foreign affairs, Margaret was a resourceful stateswoman, carefully maintaining her country's neutrality while continuing to recover lost Danish territory. To a large extent, she was able to realize her primary goals of creating a unified kingdom and sustaining Scandinavian sovereignty in the face of continued German territorial expansion. Although the tripartite union ended in 1523, the union between Sweden and Norway continued for over four centuries until 1814. Margaret died aboard her ship in the Flensburg Harbor at the age of fifty-nine.

◆ The young woman who became a national heroine by decisively turning the tide of the **Hundred Years' War (1337–1453)** in France's favor, was the daughter of a Domrémy farmer, **Jacques d'Arc**, and his wife **Isabelle de Vouthon**. A pious child, **ST. JOAN OF ARC** (in French **Sainte Jeanne d'Arc**) was thirteen years old when she had her first vision. According to legend, she first heard the voice of God in her father's garden, and over the next five years, saints Catherine, Margaret, and Michael the Archangel also appeared to her. At that time, the armies of the English **King Henry VI (1421–1471)** occupied all of northern France, including **Reims**, the traditional site of French coronations. The voices commanded her to liberate Reims so the dauphin Charles (later **Charles VII, 1403–1461**) could be crowned king.

In 1429, when Joan was sixteen, the English laid siege to **Orleans**, prompting her to seek an urgent audience with Charles, who met privately with her for two hours. She told him: "I am God's messenger, sent to tell you that you are the true heir to France and the king's son." After her claims were certified by a board of Roman Catholic Church theologians, she was sent to **Tours** to assemble an army. Dressed in a man's white armor, she carried a sword emblazoned with five crosses and a banner with a painting of the king of heaven holding an orb and the motto "Jesus Maria."

After Joan's troops entered Orleans on April 30, they stormed the Bastille of Augustine and captured Tourelles. Joan herself planted the first scaling ladder and was wounded in the shoulder. When Charles VII was crowned king on July 14, Joan, nicknamed the **Maid of Orleans**, stood proudly by his side. Following other successful defeats of the British, Joan was ennobled on December 29 in recognition of what she had done for her country.

The following year, learning that the British had recaptured **Compiègne** in preparation to take Paris, Joan mounted a campaign but failed and was taken prisoner. The English, hoping to destroy her influence and discredit Charles, turned her over to a Church court in **Rouen** for trial in January 1431. After a fourteen-month interrogation, she was judged guilty on twelve points that found her visions had been faked, censured her use of masculine dress and, most damning of all, condemned as heresy her belief that she was directly responsible to God rather than the Church. On May 30, Joan was burned at the stake in the Old Market Square at Rouen. Gazing intently at a cross she held as the flames engulfed her, she was heard to cry out "Jesus." In 1456, the Church annulled the judgment that had sentenced her to die. In 1920, Joan was canonized by **Pope Benedict XV**. Today, she is honored as the patron saint of France.

The daughter of **Juan II of Castile** and **Isabella of Portugal, ISABELLA I** was raised near Avila. At age thirteen, she was brought to the court of her half brother, **King Henry IV**. Although Henry tried to arrange a marriage for her, she insisted on making her own choice, and in 1469 she wed **Ferdinand of Aragón (1452–1516)**.

When Henry died in 1474, succession to the throne was contested by his daughter, **Juana la Beltraneja (1462–1530)**. On her behalf, her uncle **Alfonso V** of Portugal invaded Castile but was defeated in 1479, and Juana withdrew her claim. In the same year, Ferdinand succeeded to the throne of **Aragón**, becoming **Ferdinand II**. Isabella and Ferdinand's union brought the two main Spanish kingdoms together under a joint rule, which laid the foundation for Spain's future greatness as a world power.

Isabella embarked on a reform program to reduce the power of rebellious nobles by resurrecting medieval laws that allowed her to confiscate their lands. She restored the national currency, set up a national police force and army, codified laws, and organized courts in large cities. A supporter of education, she founded a new palace school and became a patron for Spanish and Flemish musicians and artists.

Known as the "Catholic Monarchs," Isabella and Ferdinand allowed the Roman Catholic Church to set up the **Inquisition** in Andalusia in 1478, beginning a dark chapter in Spanish history. Designed as a church tribunal charged with rooting out religious heresy, the Inquisition ultimately expelled over 170,000 Moors (Jews) from Spain. Although Isabella did this to unite Spain under one religion, the expulsion of many of the country's leading intellectuals and scientists proved to be more of a loss than a gain. Isabella and Ferdinand then joined forces to conquer the kingdom of **Granada**, which had been under Muslim rule for several centuries. After a ten-year campaign, in which Isabella personally took part by raising funds while traveling with her five children, Granada fell in 1492, and the Moors were driven from Spain.

In 1492, hoping to secure riches for her country and souls for her church, Isabella gave Italian explorer **Christopher Columbus (1451–1506)** financial support for his venture to find a route to the Far East by sailing west. However, when Columbus returned to Spain with natives he had taken as slaves, she ordered them freed. Only three days before she died in 1504 at the age of fifty-three, Isabella's last official act was to insist that the natives in the New World be treated fairly.

Described by many historians as one of the most beloved queens in English history, **CATHERINE OF ARAGÓN** was the daughter of **Ferdinand II** and **Isabella I** of Spain. She left Spain in 1501 to marry **Arthur**, the eldest son of **Henry VII (1457–1509)**. When Arthur died in 1502, a papal dispensation allowed her to become engaged to his brother, **Henry VIII (1491–1547)**, whom she married after he succeeded his father to the throne in 1509.

For many years, their relationship was a happy one. A woman of considerable education and culture, Catherine was a capable ruler while Henry was absent during the French campaigns (1511–1514), overseeing Britain's defense against the Scots, who were defeated at the Battle of Flodden in 1513. A great patron of education, she contributed funds for lecturers at the universities at Oxford and Cambridge and financially supported needy scholars. She also enjoyed close friendships with many of

the leading intellectuals of the day, including **Sir Thomas More (1478–1535)**, whom Henry later beheaded because of his refusal to sanction his divorce from Catherine.

Five of Catherine's six children had died, and the crown was left with only one surviving female heir, **Mary I (1516–1558)**. Henry VIII moved to annul his marriage to Catherine so he could remarry, based on his need to produce a male heir and avoid a civil war over succession to the throne. He was also infatuated with the younger and more beautiful **Anne Boleyn (c. 1507–1536)**. When the Catholic Church refused to grant his petition, Henry broke with Rome and established a new church, the **Church of England**. Fearful of alienating Catherine's nephew **Charles V** of Spain, Pope Clement delayed his decision on Henry's annulment request for seven years, until 1534. In the meantime, despite death threats and humiliations, Catherine courageously refused to give up her title of queen for princess dowager and retire to a convent. She also challenged the court hearing that Henry organized in 1529 to declare their marriage invalid on the grounds of consanguinity—the fact that she had previously been married to his brother. In 1533, Henry secretly wed Anne Boleyn and convened his own court to grant his request for annulment.

Catherine was then separated from her daughter Mary, whom she never saw again, and she was held a virtual prisoner on small estates until her death at the age of fifty-one. Despite the hardship of her last years, Catherine fared far better than Anne. After only 1,000 days as queen, during which time she produced a female heir (**Elizabeth I**, see no. 19), Anne was beheaded in 1536 by her husband so he could marry yet another woman.

◆ Queen of France from 1547 to 1559 and mother of the last three Valois kings, **CATHERINE DE' MEDICI** was a major force in French politics for more than thirty years during the prolonged period of religious wars between 1562 and 1598, and she was the mastermind of the worst mass killing in French history. She was born in Florence, Italy, the daughter of Florentine ruler **Lorenzo de' Medici**, called **Lorenzo the Magnificent**. In a marriage arranged by her uncle **Pope Clement VII**, she was wed at the age of fourteen to the Duke of Orleans, who later became **King Henry II** of France. Though she exercised little authority during her husband's reign and the reign of her eldest son **Francis II**, who was king for only a year before his death in 1560, she ruled on behalf of her second son **Charles IX** until his death in 1574. Catherine devoted most of her energy to preserving the power of her throne. To this end, she tried to maintain a balance between the Protestant Huguenots, who were led by **Admiral Gaspard de Coligny (1519–1572)**, and the Roman Catholics, whose power was concentrated in the House of Guise. A Catholic herself, Catherine neither wanted the Huguenots to dominate nor did she wish to see them crushed as they served as an effective counterbalance to limit the power of the Guise family. Her policies proved unsuccessful, and a series of religious civil wars erupted in 1562.

Her political aspirations also affected her family's personal lives. In 1560, she arranged for her daughter **Elizabeth of Valois (1545–1568)** to become the third wife of Spain's Catholic king, **Philip II (1527–1598)**. She also found it advantageous to have her daughter **Margaret of Valois (1553–1615)** marry the Protestant Henry of Navarre, later **Henry IV (1553–1610)** of France. However, Catherine had become worried about the growing influence that Huguenot leader Coligny exerted upon her son Charles.

After an assassination attempt on Coligny failed, Catherine planned an attack on prominent Huguenot leaders when they were gathered in Paris for her daughter's wedding. The carnage began at dawn on August 24, 1572, and over the next two days, 20,000 Huguenots, including Coligny, were murdered in what would come to be known as the **Massacre of St. Bartholomew's Day**. The mass killings continued across France, with the final death toll estimated at 50,000.

Catherine's power declined somewhat after her third son **Henry III (1574–1589)** ascended the throne, and she died in Blois, France, shortly before Henry was assassinated, ending the Valois line.

The forty-five-year reign of the charismatic and popular **QUEEN ELIZABETH I** ushered in an era of national achievement and economic prosperity that established England as an international power, known as the Elizabethan Age. Born in Greenwich, England, she was the daughter of **Henry VIII (1491–1547)** and his second wife, **Anne Boleyn (1507–1536)**. After her mother was executed and her parents' marriage was invalidated so her father could remarry, she was declared illegitimate. In 1544, her succession was restored by Parliament behind her half siblings **Edward (1537–1553)** and **Mary I (1516–1558)**.

When she became queen in 1558, Elizabeth moved to settle religious unrest. She reverted to Protestantism and had Parliament pass laws that formed the doctrinal basis for the Church of England which, by the **Elizabethan Settlement (1559)**, became England's official church. She supported the Protestant cause in Scotland, and when her Roman Catholic cousin **Mary, Queen of Scots (1542–1587)** sought refuge in England after being forced to abdicate, Elizabeth faced one of her most delicate political crises. Since Mary was next in line for the throne, Catholic nobles considered her the rightful English heir and plotted to usurp Elizabeth, forcing the queen to first imprison and later execute Mary in 1587.

Elizabeth instituted currency reforms, employment laws, and measures providing relief for the poor. She also showed a characteristic shrewdness of judgment when she appointed **Sir William Cecil (1520–1598)** as her chief secretary. A practical thinker like Elizabeth, he advised her to maintain a balance of power with France and Spain. Thus, for her entire life, despite Parliamentary pressure, Elizabeth continued to refuse all offers of marriage, declaring herself to be the **Virgin Queen**.

Elizabeth's domination of the era that bears her name was due in great part to the reawakening of the nationalistic fervor that she inspired. With peace, England was able to turn its energies to developing industries and strengthening its economy. Through the exploits of adventurers such as **Sir Francis Drake (c. 1540–1596)**, England increased its colonial holdings and became a great maritime power, and in 1588, was able to defeat the **Spanish Armada**. A new currency was introduced that stabilized prices and restored confidence in England. Literature and arts flourished, producing some of England's most renowned writers, such as **William Shakespeare (1564–1616)**.

Elizabeth died in London at the age of seventy. Today, she is still considered to be one of the greatest rulers in the history of England.

In the **Ndongo** tribe she was called **Nzinga Mbande**, but the name given to her by the Portuguese and in popular use today in the **People's Republic of Angola** is **QUEEN NZINGA**. A true warrior queen, she united the people of Ndongo, **Matamba, Congo, Casnje, Dembos, Kissama**, and the **Central Pianalto**, and she also succeeded in creating the greatest alliance of tribes ever formed to fight against the forces of foreign colonization in Angola. Daughter of a Ndongo **Ngola**, or king, Nzinga lived in central West Africa, where Christian missionaries arrived in 1483. Later came Portuguese traders who were primarily interested in supplying slaves to Brazilian plantations and mines. In 1576, the Portuguese extended their influence to the city of Luanda, and Portugal appointed governors to enforce colonial law. Thus began a century of war that, although ultimately won by the Portuguese, made Nzinga a national heroine.

In return for guaranteed autonomy,

tribal chiefs often sold members of rival tribes to slave traders. When the Portuguese exiled her brother for demanding total self-rule, Nzinga skillfully negotiated his release. She even agreed to be baptized, taking the name **Anna de Sousa** in honor of the incoming governor.

In 1624, when her brother died and she became queen, Nzinga resumed her tribal religion. The Portuguese, seeking to replace her with a ruler more loyal to their cause, declared war on her. She immediately allied with the Casnje, effectively closing off all slave routes. In 1630, she joined forces with the fierce **Jagas** of Matamba and gained their respect as a strong leader by participating in many of their traditional rituals dressed in men's clothing.

After forging a pan-African alliance of tribes, Nzinga began leading raids against the Portuguese, freeing many Africans destined for lives of servitude in the New World. In 1641, she drew the Portuguese troops so far inland that Luanda was seized from the Portuguese by the Dutch. However, despite victories in 1643, 1647, and 1648, she was forced to sign a peace treaty in 1654 to free her sister **Mukambu**, whom the Portuguese held captive.

About two hundred years later, American abolitionists cited Nzinga's bravery and intelligence to disprove arguments that African American slaves were inferior to whites. Immediately after Angola became independent from Portugal on November 11, 1975, the new government named a street after Nzinga in downtown Luanda. Contemporary Angolan textbooks praise her heroic career: "Even if she was not successful then, her great dream did not disappear. Her idea of a union of the Angolan people in its struggle against colonialism is today realized."

POCAHONTAS, whose Indian name **Matoaka** means "playful one," was the youngest daughter of **Chief Powhatan (c. 1550–1618)**, chief of the Powhatan empire, which consisted of a confederacy of Algonquin Native American tribes residing in the Tidewater region of Virginia. She played a key role in helping the first permanent English settlement in America, **Jamestown Colony**, flourish during its early years.

Located on an island in the James River southeast of present-day Richmond, Jamestown was first settled in 1607 by a group led by investors of the **London Company**, one of whom was **John Smith (1579–1631)**. As one story tells it, on one of his expeditions to map the surrounding area, Smith was taken captive by warriors from Chief Powhatan's tribe but was saved from being clubbed to death when twelve-year-old Pocahontas interceded. After this, Pocahontas helped to establish trade between her tribe and the settlers. This story first appeared in Smith's *Generall Historie of Virginia* (1624) and was later romanticized in a novel titled *Captain Smith and Princess Pocahontas* (1805).

Regardless of whether the Smith incident happened or not, relations between the Native Americans and the settlers deteriorated. In 1612, Pocahontas was taken hostage by **Captain Samuel Argall** and held in exchange for English prisoners and materials that had been seized by the Native Americans. During this time, at her request, she learned the English language and was baptized a Christian, taking the name **Rebecca**. She also met **John Rolfe (1585–1622)**, a planter ten years her senior, who had come to the colony in 1610. Rolfe is credited with introducing the cultivation of the **tobacco plant** to America.

Upon her marriage to Rolfe in 1614, Pocahontas's father gave the couple land, and their union ushered in eight years of peace for the Jamestown Colony. In 1616, Rolfe took his wife to England, where she was presented at court to **King James I (1556–1625)**. Dressed in finery and able to speak English, those at court saw Pocahontas as proof that the New World could indeed be "civilized" and made a hospitable place for settlers. On the eve of her return home, Pocahontas died of smallpox and was buried in the chapel of the parish church in Gravesend, England. John Rolfe returned to America, where he became a member of Virginia's first Council of State. Over the years, many prominent Virginians have claimed descent from his and Pocahontas's son, **Thomas Rolfe**.

◆ **LADY MARY MONTAGU**, the pioneer of smallpox inoculation in Europe, was a prodigious writer of letters, diaries, and poetry. Born in London, England, and the eldest child of **Evelyn Pierrepont, Duke of Kingston**, she educated herself with her father's library. In order to avoid an arranged marriage, she eloped in 1712 with **Edward Montagu (1678–1761)**, who later served as the English ambassador in Constantinople, Turkey, from 1716 to 1718.

Outspoken and forceful, Montagu's writings are considered to be among the most important literary documents from eighteenth-century England. Her ongoing feud with satirist **Alexander Pope (1688–1744)** only added to her notoriety. While living in Turkey, she wrote letters chronicling her life in the Middle East, which were published after her death in 1763. She also wrote a volume of poetry, *Town Eclogues* (1747). In 1803, her Turkish letters and other writings about English life and her travels on the continent were collected in *Works*.

During Montagu's lifetime, smallpox killed 45,000 people annually in Great Britain alone. In Turkey, she observed the procedure of **variolation**, whereby fluids from the victim of an attack of smallpox were inserted with a needle into the veins of an uninfected person. Convinced of the efficacy of this procedure, upon her return to England, she had her daughter inoculated. She also interested **Caroline, princess of Wales** in the procedure, and under Mary's direction, experiments were carried out on prisoners. After these tests proved successful, the practice of inoculation spread rapidly throughout Britain, despite opposition from medical professionals. To counter these attacks, Montagu anonymously published a tract entitled *Plain Account of the Inoculating of the Smallpox. By a Turkey Merchant* (1722).

By proving her theory that inoculation with mild smallpox could provide immunity from a serious case, Mary Montagu paved the way for public acceptance of inoculation in Europe. Her early work on variolation constituted the first step toward formulation of the theory that germs cause disease.

In failing health, and at the behest of her daughter Mary, the countess of Bute, whose husband was then prime minister, Mary Montagu returned to London, where she died in August 1762.

GABRIELLE-ÉMILIE LE TONNELIER DE BRETEUIL, a mathematician and Newtonian scientist, was born in France, the daughter of the **Baron of Preuilly**, chief of protocol at the French court. Because Émilie at five feet nine inches towered over most of her male contemporaries (she was a head taller than the philosopher **Voltaire (1694–1778)**), her parents were convinced she would never marry, and so they provided her with the best possible education.

At nineteen, Émilie married the **Marquis Florent Claude du Châtelet-Lomont**. Her social position enabled her to hire the greatest scientists of the time to tutor her in advanced physics and mathematics. With the rise of the Paris café society in the 1730s, Châtelet—disguised as a man because the only women allowed in such establishments were courtesans—was able to penetrate the exclusively male scientific network.

After meeting Voltaire in 1733, the two remodeled one of her husband's run-down estates at Cirey by transforming its great hall into a fully equipped laboratory. Châtelet conducted experiments on **Isaac Newton's (1643–1727)** optics, and her laboratory became a center for Newtonian science. She is credited with influencing Voltaire to change his focus from writing plays to studying physics and metaphysics. In 1736, they collaborated on *Elements de la Philosophie de Newton*, a popular account of Newton's theories.

Châtelet believed that Newton's purely scientific, materialistic philosophy did not offer a complete explanation and that scientific theory demanded a foundation in metaphysics. For this reason, she incorporated theories of natural philosophy by **Gottfried Leibniz (1646–1716)** in her *Institutions de Physique*, an updated introductory physics text for her son. Following its publication in

1740, younger scientists flocked to Cirey to study with her.

The culmination of Châtelet's scientific work was her two-volume translation of Newton's *Principia*. It also included her annotations, the first part of which was strictly mathematical and the second part a six-chapter, greatly improved revision of *Elements*. After its publication in 1759, ten years after Châtelet's death, Newton's scientific method became an established part of the **French Enlightenment**. Even today, her work remains the only French translation of Newton's book. A few days after giving birth to a daughter at Luneville in September 1749, she died of a pulmonary embolism at the age of forty-two.

As empress of Russia (1762–1796), the gifted and ambitious **CATHERINE THE GREAT** continued the work of Westernization and expansion begun by **Peter the Great** and helped shape the modern state of Russia. Born **Sophie Friederike Auguste, Prinzessin von Anhalt-Zerbst** in Stettin (now Szczecin), Poland, she was wed to Grand Duke **Peter of Holstein-Gottorp (Peter III, 1728–1762)** in 1745. Within months of succeeding to the throne, the disagreeable and unstable Peter had aroused so much resentment that his palace guards overthrew him and placed Catherine on the throne. Rather than rule for her seven-year-old son Paul (later **Paul I, 1754–1801**), she declared herself queen in July 1762.

Influenced by reading works of the **Enlightenment**, Catherine was determined to make Russian society as cultured as that of Paris or Berlin. She corresponded with a number of French writers, including **Voltaire (1694–1778)**, and employed experts to collect art and antiquities. Under her direction,

St. Petersburg became one of the cultural centers of Europe. She also strengthened Russia's economy by abolishing trade restrictions, and she promoted the development of underpopulated areas by encouraging settlement.

Although Catherine attempted to apply Enlightenment ideas to domestic reform, most of her new laws were designed to win support from the nobles. She exempted them from military service and expanded their rights over serfs, a system frequently used by rulers in Europe prior to the **French Revolution (1789–1799)**, a tactic that has since been coined **benevolent despotism**. As a result, peasant unrest grew, culminating in a massive peasant revolt in 1773 that was crushed by military force. To revise the **Code of Laws of 1649**, Catherine worked for two years on an *Instruction*, which would provide equal protection under the law and pursue crime prevention rather than harsh punishment—a system far ahead of its time. In 1767, she convened a Legislative Commission to encode it into law. Unfortunately, commission members became bogged down in self-interests and a year later she disbanded it. However, her 1775 reorganization of provincial administrations did prove successful. She also founded a medical college and the first Russian schools for girls.

Catherine's foreign policy was aimed at expanding Russian holdings, and judged in this context, it was a success. As a result of two wars with Turkey (1768–1774 and 1787–1791), she gained control of the Crimea and access to the Black Sea and the Dardanelles Strait. By taking part with Prussia and Austria in the three partitions of Poland (1772, 1793, 1795), she annexed a vast amount of territory on Russia's western border.

◆ **CAROLINE HERSCHEL** was one of the most famous and admired women astronomers in history, and her work helped to open the field of astronomy to other women. Born into a large family of musicians in Hanover, Germany, she went to England at age twenty-two to train as a singer and assume the role of housekeeper for her brother, astronomer **William Herschel (1738–1822)**. After discovering the planet Uranus in 1781, William was appointed King's astronomer, and Caroline became his assistant.

While other astronomers had to confine their observations to closer objects such as the planets, William's continual improvements in the magnification capabilities of his telescopes enabled him to identify distant stars. Often scanning the heavens through the night and spending their days making calculations, William and Caroline jointly founded **sidereal astronomy**—the study of stars—and advanced astronomy from a science of just the solar system to a science of stellar systems. Between 1783 and 1802, they documented 2,500 now nebulae and star clusters. Eventually, they also discovered 1,000 double stars.

During independent observations in 1783, Caroline discovered three nebulae, and in August 1786, she became the first woman to discover a comet. Over the next eleven years, she found ten more comets. In 1787, the king granted both Herschels additional funds for their work, which marked the first time a woman was appointed as an official assistant to the court astronomer.

In 1797, Caroline completed the *Catalogue of 860 Stars Observed by Flamsteed*, as well as a catalogue of 561 stars which had accidentally been omitted from the *British Catalogue*. Both were published by the **Royal Astronomical Society** in 1798.

At the age of seventy-five, she completed a formidable work on the positions of some 2,500 nebulae titled *A Catalogue of the Nebulae Which Have Been Observed by William Herschel in a Series of Sweeps*, for which she received the **Gold Medal** of the Royal Astronomical Society in 1828. In 1835, the Society voted unanimously to bestow honorary membership on the two leading women scientists of the early nineteenth century: Caroline Herschel and **Mary Fairfax Somerville** (see no. 31). After William's death in 1822, Caroline returned to Hanover, where she lived until her own death at age ninety-seven.

◆ **Eli Whitney (1765–1825)** is generally given sole credit for the invention of the **cotton gin**, a machine that revolutionized farming in the American South and profoundly affected the history of the region. However, his friend and benefactress, **CATHARINE LITTLEFIELD GREENE**, was actually the co-inventor. The daughter of a prominent Rhode Island family, she married American Revolutionary War **General Nathanael Greene (1742–1786)**. Soon after the Greenes and their five children moved to **Mulberry Grove**, a plantation on Georgia's Savannah River, the patriarch died.

During a vacation in 1792, Greene met Whitney, who was traveling to the South to become a tutor. When this job fell through, she invited him to stay at her home. Whitney, who loved to work with his hands, soon displayed exceptional mechanical talent. He devised a new part for Greene's embroidery frame and built toys for her children.

During a gathering at Greene's plantation, a group of local planters discussed the future of agriculture in the South and agreed the crop of choice was cotton. However, removing cotton seeds was such tedious work because it took one person an entire day to produce a cleaned pound. Greene told the planters to talk to Whitney about their problem.

For the next several weeks, Whitney worked on the design and construction of the cotton gin, a machine consisting of a wooden cylinder encircled by a row of slender spikes. However, his initial model was significantly flawed. Although it could pull the seeds from the cotton, the loose seeds clogged the roller. When he talked to Greene about his dilemma, she recommended that he install a brush and gave him one from her kitchen. Once installed, the revolving brush successfully cleaned the spikes, pushing the seeds into a separate compartment. The gin, which was cranked by hand, could clean up to fifty pounds of cotton a day.

Whitney went into partnership with Greene's plantation manager, **Phineas Miller (d. 1803)**, whom Greene married in 1796. Although the men received a patent, they were unable to meet the demand for the machines, and country blacksmiths began to pirate their simple design. During the ensuing lengthy and costly patent fight, it was Greene who provided the funds for the men to stay in business, eventually selling her plantation in 1800 to pay legal fees. Whitney finally won full title to the cotton gin in 1807. However, neither he nor Greene ever realized much profit from their invention, which had turned cotton into the most important cash crop in the South.

When **MARIE-ANNE PIERETTE PAULZE** was fourteen, her father arranged a marriage with **Antoine Lavoisier (1743-1794)**, a man who was twice her age and already an established chemist. For the next twenty-five years, the Lavoisiers collaborated continuously. Their work on heat and fire brought about a fundamental shift in the study of chemistry by replacing old beliefs of **alchemy** with a new system of scientific principles, thus laying the groundwork for modern chemistry.

Marie first learned Latin and English so she could translate chemical studies. Her collection of translations with original comments was titled *Annales de chimie et de physique*, which were published in 1792. She also illustrated her husband's numerous publications, assisted with experiments, took notes, kept laboratory records, and maintained their scientific correspondence.

Completing some of the earliest known quantitative experiments, the Lavoisiers were able to demonstrate that burning is a process involving the combination of a substance with a portion of the atmosphere—an element that Antoine later named **oxygen**. These findings are described in *Méthode de nomenclature chimique*, the first modern chemistry text. In it, the term **element** is redefined as being a simple substance that cannot be broken down by any known method of chemical analysis. Marie's copperplate illustrations, original drawings, and watercolors for this book survive as her most famous contributions.

Marie and her husband also discovered the **law of conservation of matter**, which states that the weight of the products from a chemical reaction must equal the weight of the reagents. Their studies of animal metabolism demonstrated the role of oxygen in animal and plant respiration.

After both her husband and father were guillotined in 1794 during the **French Revolution (1789–1799)**, Marie completed *Mémoires de chimie*, an eight-volume work, and published it under her husband's name in 1805. The widow spent her last years as a successful businesswoman and philanthropist, but it was increasingly difficult to continue scientific work alone. She died in 1836 at the age of seventy-eight.

◆ Considered by historians as the first modern feminist, **MARY WOLLSTONECRAFT** was born in England during the Age of Reason, a period of revolution and change in America and France. Her childhood was unhappy and marked by abuse, and she left home at twenty-one to earn a living on her own as a teacher and governess.

Following the modest success of her first book, a novel titled *Mary: A Fiction* (1788), she moved to London and supported herself as a writer, reader, and translator. There she became involved with a radical circle of intellectuals, with whom she dined each Thursday—revolutionary **Thomas Paine (1737–1809)**, poet **William Blake (1757–1827)**, and chemist **Joseph Priestley (1733–1804)** among others. Shunning the traditional restraints that normally bound women, she soon made a name for herself by actively defending the most progressive ideas of her day. Her pioneer work, *A Vindication of the Rights of Women* (1792), which was based on the premise that freedom and equality applied to women as well as men, caused an immediate sensation and made her one of the most famous—and controversial—women in Europe. Wollstonecraft also insisted that governments were obliged to provide an education for all citizens, with equal access guaranteed for women, arguing that if a woman "be not prepared by education to become the companion of man, she will stop the progress of knowledge."

Wollstonecraft also asserted that a marriage in which the wife was a mere adornment, a bearer of children, or used only for physical release was unacceptable. She proposed intellectual companionship and equality between partners. These crusading ideas would not be repeated, much less acted upon, for over 100 years.

In 1797, she married political philosopher **William Godwin (1756–1836)**. That same year she gave birth to their daughter, Mary (later **Mary Shelley (1797–1851)**), author of the famous horror story *Frankenstein*, and died soon after from an infection.

Wollstonecraft's other works include *Original Stories from Real Life* (1788) and *A Vindication of the Rights of Man* (1793). Her letters were published in *Memoirs of the Author of the Rights of Women* (1798). For an excellent novelization of her life and times, see Frances Sherwood's *Vindication* (1993).

After the fall of the **Bastille** in 1789 during the **French Revolution (1789–1799)**, the streets of Paris became a chaotic, dangerous place, so thirteen-year-old **MARIE-SOPHIE GERMAIN's** parents confined her to their home. Seeking refuge in her father's extensive library, she came upon the story of the death of **Archimedes (c. 287–212 BCE)**. The Greek mathematician, completely absorbed in his study of a geometric figure in the sand, failed to respond to an invading Roman soldier's questions and was speared to death. Inspired, Germain decided to learn all she could about what had so fascinated Archimedes—mathematics.

Germain's parents, however, were concerned that such "brainwork" was not healthy for a woman and actively discouraged her. Undeterred, Germain often studied through the night, teaching herself differential calculus. Denied admittance at the newly opened École Polytechnique because she was a woman, she obtained lecture notes on chemistry from an analysis class taught by **Joseph-Louis Lagrange (1736–1813)** in 1795. She then submitted a paper to Lagrange under the pseudonym of "LeBlanc." Lagrange was so impressed with the paper that, after learning who the author was, he went to Germain's home to congratulate her. Thus encouraged, Germain began to correspond with several scholars and scientists. She was particularly interested in the number theory of **Carl Gauss (1777–1855)**, and for three years, she exchanged letters with him using the name "Monsieur LeBlanc." When the French army invaded his German hometown, she asked the commanding general—an old family friend—to spare Gauss's life. When Gauss learned Germain's true identity, he was even more impressed and shared her work with his colleagues.

After physicist **Ernst Chladni** demonstrated how patterns could be reproduced by sprinkling sand on a plate and striking the plate with a violin bow, interest in the resonant vibration of elastic bodies was renewed. The French Academy called for papers that would explain and predict the unusual patterns that sand or powder would make on reverberating, flexible surfaces. In 1816, Germain won the Academy's grand prize for her mathematical formula on the **law of vibrating elastic surfaces**. Her formula was subsequently used by scientists to solve practical problems in building construction, making possible the building of structures such as the **Eiffel Tower**. Sophie Germain spent the remainder of her life independently working on number theory, and she died of cancer at the age of fifty-five in Paris.

◆ Devout Society of Friends (Quaker) minister and prison reformer **ELIZABETH GURNEY** was born in Norfolk, England, the fourth of twelve children of a prosperous banker. The Gurneys were "wide Quakers," meaning that the women did not wear the traditional gray dress and bonnet ensemble, and the men also did not wear wide-brimmed hats.

A turning point in Elizabeth's life occurred when, at the age of eighteen, she met American evangelist **William Savery** after he spoke at a Norwich religious revival meeting. Following this, she became a "plain Friend," adopting their traditional gray costume and becoming more orthodox.

In 1800, Elizabeth married **John Fry**, a London merchant, and in 1809, she became a Quaker minister. She already had eight of her ten children when she first visited **Newgate Prison** in 1813 at the urging of a clergyman from America who had gone to Newgate to work with the prisoners. Appalled at the squalid living conditions, particularly for the women, he sought Fry's assistance. She later said that she had found "half naked women, struggling together... with the most boisterous violence... I felt as if I were going into a den of wild beasts."

Known as an effective public speaker, Fry often read the Bible aloud to an overflowing room of women. Said a fellow minister who witnessed one of these sessions: "There they sat in respectful silence, every eye fixed upon...the gentle lady... never till then, and never since then, have I heard anyone read as Elizabeth Fry read..."

Besides her ministerial duties, Fry also began an aggressive campaign for the humane treatment of women prisoners and of convicts who were transported to New South Wales, Australia, which at that time was being used as a British penal colony. She sought to keep men separate from women, to seek employment for prisoners, and to classify and segregate the more violent cases from the weaker individuals. She also founded a prison school and a **Prisoners' Aid Society** in 1817.

After giving compelling testimony to the 1818 Royal Commission, Fry toured the British Isles in the 1820s, inspecting facilities and outlining necessary improvements, and founding women's associations and prison reform groups. Having become famous throughout Britain, she traveled throughout Europe to meet with heads of state. In 1838, **King Louis Philippe (1773–1850)**, who was also called the **Citizen King**, invited her to France to examine French prisons. Her report led to penal reforms there. During her lifetime, Fry also worked to raise the standards, training, and status of nurses; to improve educational facilities for women; and to secure housing and employment for London's poor.

◆ Upon her death in 1872, *The London Post* acclaimed her as the **"queen of nineteenth-century science."** A heroine in both scientific and activist circles, **MARY FAIRFAX SOMERVILLE** was an outspoken supporter of women's suffrage and was the first to sign a petition for women's rights presented to Parliament by **John Stuart Mill (1806–1873).** Her enduring scientific legacy and widespread popularity was due to her ability to explain the prevailing state of science in terms that educated laymen could readily understand.

The only daughter of a Scottish admiral, Somerville grew up in the coastal village of Burtisland. Although her formal education consisted of one year at boarding school, her uncle inspired her with stories of women scholars throughout the ancient world. She also studied *Elements* by **Euclid (c. 3rd–2nd century BCE)** and an algebra text she obtained from her brother's tutor. Soon she was reading *Principles* by **Sir Isaac Newton (1642–1727)**, and she went on to study botany, meteorology, astronomy, higher mathematics, and physics.

After publishing several scientific papers, her translation of *Traité de mécanique céleste* by **Pierre-Simon Laplace (1749–1827)**, titled *Mechanism of the Heavens*, appeared in 1831. *Preliminary Dissertation*, her addition to the original text, outlined the basic mathematics a reader needed to understand Laplace's concepts, the history of the subject, and her explanation of the book with original drawings, diagrams, and mathematical calculations. *Mechanism* remained a standard text in higher mathematics and astronomy for the rest of the century. In her book *Physical Sciences* (1834), Somerville "tried to make the laws by which the material world is governed more familiar to my countrywomen." *Sciences* went through ten editions over the next forty years and was translated into several languages. It proved popular with scientists and the public.

In 1838, Somerville published her most successful book, *Physical Geography*. It was a purely descriptive work and contained many of her political views, such as her stance against slavery. Honorary memberships in the Royal Astronomical Society and other European organizations were offered to her. Her last book, *On Molecular and Microscopic Science*, published in 1869 when she was eighty-nine, ranged from atomic theory to a catalog of plants. Mary Somerville died peacefully in her sleep at the age of ninety-two in Naples, Italy.

◆ After crowning himself king of France in 1804, **Napoleon Bonaparte (1769–1821)** embarked on a campaign of conquest between 1806 and 1814. Following victories against Austria (1805) and Prussia (1806), he set out to force England into submission by cutting off trade. To this end, he undertook the **Peninsular War (1808–1814)** in Spain and Portugal. It was during this campaign that eighteen-year-old **AGUSTINA OF ARAGÓN**, also known as the **Maid of Saragossa**, became a national heroine when she valiantly rallied her people during the first French siege of Saragossa (or Zaragoza in Spanish) in Spain, between June 15 and August 15, 1808. In 1807, Napoleon forced the Spanish **King Charles IV (1788–1808)** to let his troops pass through Spain to attack Portugal and provide Spanish troops. In return, he promised to divide a conquered Portugal between France and Spain. Once French troops reached Portugal's capital, however, Napoleon turned against Spain, and by March 1808, he had seized the capital.

The Spanish, realizing Napoleon's treachery, rose in revolt. Over one hundred thousand men gathered. They were brave and enthusiastic but lacked arms, organization, and commanders. Napoleon immediately counterattacked. His key targets became the ports on the eastern coast of Spain and the fortress of Saragossa, a provincial capital located on the Ebro river. In the heat of the French attack, Agustina arrived at the Portillo gate with food for the soldiers but found that many were either dead or had abandoned their posts. Picking up a match from the hand of a dead gunner, she declared that she would not leave until the battle had been won, then lit the fuse on the 620-pound cannon. Inspired by her show of bravery, soldiers returned to combat.

True to her word, Agustina remained at this front line until the French retreated two months later. In the interim, she displayed incredible bravery by rescuing the wounded while under siege and tending to their injuries without rest. One romanticized story describes how, in the thick of battle, "an unknown maiden issued from the Church of Nostra Donna de Pillas... in white raiment, a cross suspended from her neck... her eyes sparkling with supernatural luster."

Thanks in part to Agustina's leadership, Spanish forces successfully repelled the French. She became a symbol of national pride, liberty, and heroism, and she was immortalized by poet **Lord Byron (1788–1824)** in *Childe Harold's Pilgrimage* and in paintings by **Francisco de Goya (1746–1828)**.

Born among the **Lemhi Shoshone** Native American tribe of western Montana, **SACAGAWEA** was kidnapped as a teenager by the **Hidatsa**, who took her to their village on the upper Missouri in North Dakota. In 1804, she was purchased by French Canadian trader **Toussaint Charbonneau** and she became one of his two Native American wives.

The expedition led by **Meriwether Lewis (1774–1809)** and **William Clark (1770–1838)** traveled up the Missouri River from St. Louis, Missouri, in May 1804, and during a stopover at a Mandan village in South Dakota, they hired Charbonneau as an interpreter. He brought Sacagawea, who spoke Shoshone and Siouan. Shortly before the expedition set out from Fort Mandan in April 1805, she gave birth to a son, **Jean-Baptiste**. Known as "Pompey," he made the eight-thousand-mile journey in a cradleboard strapped to his mother's back.

As the sole female member of the forty-man group, Sacagawea proved invaluable. Not only did she provide expert guidance through the wilderness of Montana, but her presence was viewed as a token of peace, and she was able to communicate with the tribes they encountered through language and signs. She also introduced the use of wild plants as food, and she saved the expedition's journals after her husband accidentally capsized a canoe. Members of the expedition later praised her "resourcefulness, courage, and good humor," but said her husband had "mistreated her and was not worthy of his hire." For his services, Charbonneau was paid $503.33, but Sacagawea received nothing.

In August 1805, in the Three Forks region of Missouri in present-day Montana, Sacagawea was reunited with her brother, the tribal chief. At her request, her brother **Cameahwait** provided horses, supplies, and guides for them to use while crossing the Rocky Mountains. The expedition continued up the Clearwater, Snake, and Columbia rivers, reaching the Pacific Ocean in November 1805. On the return journey, Sacagawea accompanied Clark's party down the Yellowstone River, disembarking with her family at the mouth of the Knife River while the expedition returned to St. Louis, Missouri, in 1806.

The remainder of Sacagawea's life is uncertain. It is believed that she and her husband visited St. Louis sometime after 1806, leaving their son with Clark, who sponsored his education. One story says she died of disease in 1812, but another story reports that she lived to be nearly 100 years old. In addition to numerous memorials along the explorers' route, Sacagawea also has a river, a mountain, and a pass named in her honor.

Born on Nantucket Island, Massachusetts, **LUCRETIA COFFIN** was educated at Nine Partners, a Society of Friends (Quaker) boarding school in Poughkeepsie, New York. When she learned that the men at her school were paid twice as much as the women, she decided to become a women's rights activist. At eighteen, she married **James Mott (1788–1868)**, who had been one of her teachers and shared her views.

After 1817, Mott became prominent among the Quakers and, when the sect split into two factions in 1827, she and her husband joined the **Hicksites**—the liberal faction led by **Elias Hicks**. In 1833, the Motts helped found the **American Anti-Slavery Society**, and in 1840, they were delegates to an international antislavery convention in London. Lucretia and **Elizabeth Cady Stanton** (see no. 38), who also attended the convention, were excluded from participation by being seated behind a heavy curtain, such that they could only listen to the proceedings. Angered by this discriminatory treatment, both women vowed to devote their energies solely to the cause of equal rights for women.

In 1848, Mott and Stanton called the first **Women's Rights Convention** to "discuss the social, civil, and religious condition and rights of women." The convention, which was held at a Wesleyan chapel in Seneca Falls, New York, drew more than 100 people, both male and female. The delegates agreed that their primary goal was universal suffrage for women, and they adopted Stanton's *Declaration of Sentiments*, which was patterned on the **Declaration of Independence**. This statement was the first public demand for women's voting rights. After the convention, however, others branded the suffragists as "unfeminine" and accused them of immorality, despite the support of many prominent Americans behind the new movement. At times when suffragist leaders undertook speaking tours, they were subjected to physical violence.

Following the passage of the second **Fugitive Slave Act** in 1850, the Motts made their home a station on the **Underground Railroad**, an organization that helped slaves escape to freedom that was organized largely by **Harriet Tubman** (see no. 47). In 1866, Lucretia was named the first president of the **American Equal Rights Association**. For many years, the Motts traveled widely, lecturing on women's suffrage, temperance, and world peace. When her husband died in 1868, she took his place as president of the **Pennsylvania Peace Society**. Lucretia Mott died in her home Roadside, north of Philadelphia, at the age of eighty-seven.

♦ Many of the ideas about American education that are considered "modern" today actually originated with **CATHARINE BEECHER**, a pioneer in mathematics education and education for women. She was born in the state of New York in 1800, one of thirteen children of Presbyterian minister **Lyman Beecher (1775–1863)** and a mother who loved to solve mathematical problems. Her famous siblings include **Harriet Beecher Stowe** (see no. 37), and abolitionist **Henry Ward Beecher (1813–1887)**.

At a time when university education was not accessible for women, Beecher undertook a two-year independent study course to prepare herself for teaching at the age of twenty. She later opened the **Hartford Seminary for Girls** in Hartford, Connecticut, where her sister Harriet was first a pupil and then a teacher.

In 1832, Beecher opened the **Western Female Institute** in Cincinnati to train teachers for the vast territory of the West, and 30,000 teachers received training through this school and other organizations she set up around the country. In addition to expanding the school curriculum to include physical education classes, she was one of the first to teach home economics as a school subject. She wrote several books on "domestic science," including *A Treatise on Domestic Economy*, which explained how to systematize homemaking skills. In 1832, she became one of the first American women to write a mathematics textbook, *Arithmetic Simplified*. Her work also led her to found the **American Women's Educational Association**.

Some of Catharine Beecher's innovative ideas included: (1) dividing students below college level into smaller classes that were approximately equal in ability; (2) using the most gifted students to assist her in class; (3) limiting mathematics class size to six to ten students, as she believed this was the maximum a teacher could teach effectively; (4) having teachers teach only two or three subjects instead of all subjects; (5) encouraging teachers to use "objects of sight" (visual aids) in mathematics instruction; (6) using blackboards to work out problems—rather than having students memorize everything, as was the prevailing custom—and placing the boards all around the room, which was an advanced idea at that time; and (7) expecting students not merely to calculate the answers by rote but also to fully understand what they were doing and be able to communicate their reasoning in mathematical language.

Born in Hampden, Maine, and the daughter of an itinerant preacher, pioneer prison reformer **DOROTHEA DIX** described her poverty-stricken childhood as a "time of loneliness and despair." At twelve, she ran away from home and persuaded her grandmother in Boston to take her in. For fifteen years, she operated schools in the homes of her grandmother and aunt. She also wrote several children's books, including *Conversations on Common Things*, which reached its sixtieth edition by 1869.

The turning point in Dix's life occurred when she volunteered to teach a Sunday school class in an East Cambridge jail, where she was horrified to discover that people with mental illnesses were being kept in unheated cells, even in the most frigid weather. The jailer explained to Dix that the "insane" didn't feel changes in temperature and refused to honor her pleas to provide heat. Dix then took the case to court and won.

Over the next two years, Dix visited jails, workhouses, almshouses, and hospitals all over Massachusetts, documenting their appalling conditions. In 1845, **Samuel Howe** presented her *Memorial: To the Massachusetts Legislature* report, in which Dix called the legislature's attention to the "present state of insane persons confined... in cages, closets, cellars, pens; chained, naked, beaten with rods, and lashed into obedience." Her exposé caused a public outcry, and a reform bill was passed. That same year, her book *Prison and Prison Discipline* appeared.

This success launched Dix's lifelong career as a prison reformer. She traveled state to state visiting various institutions, studying their needs and enlisting the help of philanthropists and politicians to renovate or build facilities and improve treatment. Dix also founded new hospitals or additions in five northeastern states and Canada and received authorization from state legislatures to set up state hospitals in ten other states from Maryland to Missouri.

In 1848, Dix visited the British Isles and found Scottish institutions in need of reform, so she presented a case to the advocate of Scotland. In Rome, she met with Pope Pius IX to share her concerns about Italy's inadequate facilities. He ordered the construction of a new hospital and revised rules for the care of people with mental illnesses. Before returning to the United States, Dix inspected hospitals and prisons in Austria, Belgium, France, Germany, Greece, Holland, Russia, across Scandinavia, and Turkey and recommended improvements.

In 1861, Dix was appointed superintendent of women nurses during the **American Civil War (1861–1865)**. After the war, she resumed her reform efforts until her death at age eighty-five in Trenton, New Jersey.

◆ Born in Litchfield, Connecticut, the seventh of thirteen children of Presbyterian minister **Lyman Beecher (1775–1863)**, abolitionist and author **HARRIET BEECHER STOWE's** famous siblings include her older sister, education pioneer **Catharine Beecher** (see no. 35) and abolitionist **Henry Ward Beecher (1813–1887)**. In 1832, she accompanied her father to his new post as president of Lane Theological Seminary in Cincinnati and married **Calvin Stowe**, a professor and ardent opponent of slavery, in 1836. Her first book was *The Mayflower* (1843).

For eighteen years, Stowe lived across the Ohio River from Kentucky, a slave-holding state. Moved by the despair of fugitive slaves and believing she had a religious message to deliver, she wrote a serialized tale in 40 installments for the Washington, DC-based antislavery paper *The National Era*, entitled *Uncle Tom's Cabin, or, Life Among the Lowly* about how slavery was destroying black family life. Published as a book on March 20, 1852, *Uncle Tom's Cabin* so aroused the national conscience against slavery that it served to hasten the onset of the **American Civil War (1861–1865)**. Though not a great literary work, it stands as perhaps the single most influential book in American history.

The success of *Uncle Tom's Cabin* was unprecedented. In the five years following its publication, it sold 500,000 copies in the United States and was translated into more than twenty languages. In 1853, Stowe published *A Key to Uncle Tom's Cabin*, which contained a wealth of documentary evidence to support the militant antislavery stance of her previous book. That same year, she journeyed to Europe to lecture against slavery. In 1856, another antislavery book, *Dred: A Tale of the Dismal Swamp*, appeared.

Harriet Beecher Stowe lived out her life as a woman of letters, writing several more novels and a volume of religious poetry, occasionally giving public readings of her works. She died in Hartford, Connecticut, at the age of eighty-five.

Born in Johnston, New York, as the daughter of Judge **Daniel Cady**, women's rights activist **ELIZABETH CADY STANTON** observed firsthand the tragic effects of discriminatory laws against women, which encouraged her to fight for equality. By circulating petitions, she was instrumental in the passage of an 1848 New York law granting property rights to women. Through her work in the antislavery movement, she met **Henry Stanton**, a journalist and antislavery orator. They married in 1840 and had eight children.

In 1840, Stanton began working with **Lucretia Coffin Mott** (see no. 34), and in 1848 they organized the first **Women's Rights Convention** in Seneca Falls, New York, which included many male sympathizers. Stanton, a gifted writer, drafted the *Declaration of Sentiments*—patterned after the **Declaration of Independence**—stating that men and women were created equal and demanding, for the first time publicly, that women be granted voting rights.

In 1851, Stanton began a fifty-year collaboration on antislavery and feminist causes with **Susan B. Anthony** (see no. 45), during which Stanton provided the ideas and written works and Anthony provided the oratorical and organizational talent. From 1858 to 1860, they published a weekly New York newspaper called *Revolution*, edited by Stanton, which was devoted to publicizing incidents of unequal treatment of women.

After the **American Civil War (1861–1865)**, male abolitionists voiced fears that the demands of women suffragists would jeopardize the campaign to secure voting rights for former male slaves. In response, Stanton and Anthony created the **National Woman Suffrage Association** in 1869 to deal specifically with the issue of securing national voting rights for women, of which Stanton served as president until 1892.

Besides Stanton and Anthony, the association included many other leading activists such as **Jane Addams** (see no. 60), **Clara Barton** (see no. 48), **Carrie Chapman Catt** (see no. 59), **Julia Ward Howe (1819–1910)** and **Harriet Beecher Stowe** (see no. 37). In 1888, Stanton and Anthony helped found the **International Council of Women** to coordinate suffragist efforts worldwide. In conjunction with Anthony, **Ida Harper**, and **Matilda Gage**, Stanton worked on the first three volumes of *The History of Woman Suffrage* (six volumes, 1881–1922). She died in New York City at the age of eighty-six.

◆ Born in London, England, mathematician and pioneer computer scientist **ADA BYRON** was the daughter of poet **Lord George Byron (1788–1824)** and **Annabella Milbanke**, whom Bryon once referred to as the "princess of parallelograms" because of her interest in mathematics. Shortly after her birth, Lord Byron left his family and Ada never saw him again. At age nineteen, she married the **Earl of Lovelace**.

In 1833, Lovelace and family friend **Mary Fairfax Somerville (see no. 31)** viewed a model of the **Difference Engine** in the studio of inventor and scientist **Charles Babbage (1791–1871)**. After studying finite differences—the mathematical basis of Babbage's invention—Lovelace initiated an eighteen-year correspondence with him, during which she progressed from being his student to being his collaborator. In 1842, she translated a paper by Italian mathematician **L. F. Menabrea** on the function and theory of Babbage's newest invention, the **Analytical Engine**, adding her own annotations and seven notes which greatly elaborated on the original. Lovelace's work was superior to Menabrea's, and Babbage encouraged her to publish it as a separate paper, which she did in *Taylor's Scientific Memoirs* (1843). She signed it "A. L. L." because in her day, it would have been unseemly for a noblewoman to take credit for such a work. Her identity remained secret from the public for the next thirty years.

In her notes, Lovelace made a detailed comparison of Babbage's two inventions. Whereas the Difference Engine could merely tabulate, the Analytical Engine could both tabulate and develop. She also described how to feed information into the Engine on punched cards. As in modern **computer punch cards**, the patterns of the holes corresponded to mathematical symbols. In another remarkable note, Lovelace predicted the future possibility of **computerized music**, stating that music itself is mathematical and thus adaptable to being composed by a machine.

Babbage's invention never progressed past the planning stage due to a lack of funds and the fact that his design was too far advanced for precision engineering technology of his time. However, by the mid-twentieth century, he would be recognized as the father of modern computers and Ada Lovelace as the first person to fully describe the process now known as **computer programming**. In the 1980s, in recognition of Lovelace's pioneering achievements, the U.S. Department of Defense named its new systems implementation programming language **Ada**. Ada Lovelace died of cancer at the age of thirty-six.

CHARLOTTE and **EMILY** were born in Yorkshire at Thornton, England. Their Irish father, **Patrick Brontë**, who himself was the author of two volumes of verse, served as a rector at Haworth until his death in 1861. After their mother, **Maria Branwell**, died of cancer in 1821, her sister Elizabeth came to care for the family. The children were often left alone to amuse themselves and they spent their time reading, walking the moors, and writing an enormous amount of juvenile literature. In the span of fifteen months, Charlotte wrote twenty-three "novels," which, though of no consequence now, demonstrate the depth of her creative energy.

Together with their sister **Anne (1820–1849)** and brother **Patrick Bronwell (1817–1848)**, the sisters created a series of stories about two imaginary kingdoms called Angria, which belonged to Charlotte and Bronwell, and Gondal, which was the property of Emily and Anne. One hundred handwritten chronicles about Angria,

started in 1829, still survive today, although only a few of Emily's poems from the Gondal series exist. For one year, Charlotte and Emily and their two elder sisters, **Maria (1814–1825)** and **Elizabeth (1815–1825)**, attended the Clergy Daughters' School at Cowen's Bridge. The horrors they experienced there—inadequate food and overly harsh discipline—were later described by Charlotte in *Jane Eyre*, in which she called the school **Lowood**.

In 1842, Charlotte and Emily, with the idea of eventually opening their own school, went to school in Brussels to improve their French but were quickly called home due to the death of their aunt. Charlotte later returned to Brussels, and her experience there formed the basis for her novel *Villette* (1852), a story powered by the intense loneliness of its heroine. Upon her return to Haworth, she and Emily attempted to set up a tutoring business in their home, but their advertisements failed to draw any pupils. This disappointment was compounded by their brother's complete collapse. A failed painter who had been dismissed from several positions, Bronwell became addicted to alcohol and opium.

In 1846, Charlotte discovered Emily's poems, which prompted them, along with Anne, to jointly self-publish their verses, using pseudonyms based on the letters of their first names. The volume, *Poems by Currer, Ellis, and Acton Bell*, sold two copies. Undeterred, each set about writing a novel. Charlotte's *Jane Eyre*, a portrait of a governess on a remote estate belonging to a moody, tormented man, appeared first. Later the same year, Anne's *Agnes Grey* and Emily's *Wuthering Heights* were published. Bronwell died in September 1848, succumbing to his prolonged struggle with alcoholism. Emily died in December of tuberculosis.

EMILY BRONTË

Anne died the following May of the same disease. Her second novel, *The Tenant of Wildfell Hall* (1848), which described an alcoholic's decline, contained many autobiographical elements.

Charlotte went on to complete two more novels: *Shirley* (1849), a realistic drama concerning workers and their masters in the weaving industry a generation before, and *The Professor* (1857). In 1854, she married her father's curate, Arthur Nicholls. While pregnant the following year, she died of tuberculosis.

The work of the reclusive Brontë sisters, most notably *Jane Eyre* and *Wuthering Heights*, have become enduring literary classics because their timeless themes transcend the Victorian era in which they were written. Anne Brontë's work, though less known, should not be discounted, for by her presence and interaction, she added greatly to the literary milieu in the Brontë household.

Jane Eyre, because it does not conform to the realm of conventional "women's fiction" of the time, is considered one of the most stirring depictions of feminism in English literature. *Wuthering Heights*, hauntingly grim and melancholy in tone, reveals the mystical side of Emily's personality. Both are stories of passionate love, which portray their female heroines as flaunting the traditional societal belief that women were merely the loved and not the lovers, a theme that many of their Victorian readers surely found to be a bit shocking but nonetheless irresistible.

CHARLOTTE BRONTË

Growing up in Brookfield, Massachusetts, women's rights activist **LUCY STONE** was deeply disturbed over the long hours of hard work imposed on her mother, who had been required to milk eight cows the night before Lucy was born. In order to determine if biblical scriptures approving the subjugation of women were correctly translated, she resolved to go to college to study Greek and Hebrew. After saving money for nine years, she entered Oberlin College in Ohio—then the only American institution admitting women—at age twenty-five. Because she had to work to pay tuition, she would arise at two o'clock in the morning to study. Her outspoken views rankled some of the faculty, but she graduated first in her class in 1847.

In 1848, she was hired as a lecturer for the **Anti-Slavery Society**, agreeing to appear at meetings on Saturday evenings and Sundays. During the week, she frequently lectured on women's rights. In 1855, she married the noted abolitionist **Henry Blackwell (1824–1909)**, brother of **Elizabeth Blackwell (see no. 49)**, and they issued a joint protest against the unfairness of marriage laws. As a symbol of her right to individuality, Stone, with her husband's full support, retained her maiden name after marriage. Other women who followed her example became known as **Stoners**.

In 1869, **Susan B. Anthony (see no. 45)** and **Elizabeth Cady Stanton (see no. 38)** formed the **National Woman Suffrage Association** to seek a constitutional amendment granting women the right to vote. Stone, disagreeing with their strategy, formed the **American Woman Suffrage Association** in conjunction with **Henry Ward Beecher (1813–1887)** to work toward the gradual state-by-state adoption of women's suffrage. Later that year, Wyoming became the first state to grant women the right to vote. In 1890, the Stone-Beecher organization merged with the Anthony-Stanton group to become the **National American Woman Suffrage Association**. The organization continued to work toward the goal of women's suffrage on both the state and federal levels until Congress ratified the **Nineteenth Amendment** to the U.S. Constitution in 1920, securing the right to vote for American women.

In 1870, Stone founded the *Woman's Journal*, which became the main publication of the women's suffrage movement. With the assistance of her husband, and later her daughter, she edited it until her death in 1893 at the age of seventy-six. At that time, she achieved yet another first as she became the first woman in New England to be cremated.

Born in Chivers Coton, Warwickshire, England, and daughter of an estate agent, the childhood of author and essayist **MARY ANN EVANS** was dominated by strict religious training. She attended boarding school until age seventeen when her mother's death made it necessary for her to return home to keep house for her father. Always an avid reader, she eventually rebelled against the oppressive orthodoxy and became known for her unconventional ways.

Evans' first work was a translation of *Das Leben Jesu*, a German theological work. In 1851, after traveling in Europe for two years, she wrote a book review for the *Westminster Review*. Later, as an assistant editor at the publication, she met and worked with many leading English literary figures, including **Herbert Spencer (1820–1903)**, **John Stuart Mill (1806–1873)**, and philosopher and critic **George Lewes (1817–1878)**. She and Lewes immediately fell in love. Unable to marry because Lewes' wife was insane (English law forbade a divorce under such circumstances), Evans and Lewes spent the next twenty-four years together, a mutually satisfying relationship that Evans viewed as a marriage. For his part, Lewes was extremely protective of her in later life, even shielding her from unfavorable literary reviews.

Evans began writing stories for *Blackwood's Magazine*, and several were collected and published in 1858 as *Scenes from a Clerical Life* under her new pen name of **George Eliot**, a pseudonym she employed for many years. This work made an immediate impression on the literary world and was highly praised by author **Charles Dickens (1812–1870)**, among others. There followed, in rapid succession, the publication of Evans' most well-known works: *Adam Bede* (1859), *The Mill on the Floss* (1860), and *Silas Marner* (1861). Together, these highly realistic, autobiographical depictions of Victorian country life constitute Evans' most valuable contribution to English literature and our knowledge of English social history in the mid-nineteenth century.

Evans wrote numerous other essays, books, and poems, including her novel *Middlemarch* (1871) until Lewes's death in 1878, when she became a recluse and ceased to write. These later works were also well received among her contemporaries. Of particular note is her novel *Daniel Deronda* (1876), a strongly worded indictment of anti-Semitism. In May 1880, she married American banker **John Cross**, a longtime friend, but she died in London on December 22 of that same year.

◆ A woman intensely devoted to her duties as a wife, mother, and queen, **QUEEN VICTORIA** became a living symbol of the greatness of the British Empire at the height of its glory. Her sixty-four-year reign—one of the longest in the crown's history—came to be called the **Victorian Age**, an era characterized by ardent nationalism and a return to conservative morality. Born in Kensington Palace, London, and the only child of **Edward, Duke of Kent**, who was the youngest brother of **William IV (1765–1837)** and **Mary Louisa Victoria** of Saxe-Coburg-Gotha, she succeeded her uncle to the throne at the age of eighteen when he died without an heir.

In 1840, Victoria married her cousin **Prince Albert, Duke of Saxe-CoburgGotha (1819–1861)**. Though it was an arranged marriage, it proved to be a highly romantic and rewarding one. After his death in 1861, she spent three years in total seclusion and did not appear to open Parliament until 1864. She then continued to wear black and actively mourn Albert for the rest of her life.

The first of Victoria and Albert's nine children—also named Victoria—was born in 1840 and later became the empress of Germany. Queen Victoria's first grandchild was born in 1859 and her first great-grandchild was born in 1879. By the time of her death in 1901, she had thirty-seven living great-grandchildren. Her descendants eventually ruled in Sweden, Denmark, Norway, Spain, Greece, and Russia, thus earning her the affectionate title of the **Grandmother of Europe**.

Under Albert's considerable influence, Victoria exercised her full rights as a constitutional monarch "to be consulted, the right to encourage, and the right to warn" her prime ministers. She became a strong supporter of the Conservative Party, subsequently enjoying congenial relationships with prime ministers **Sir John Peel (1788–1850)** and **Benjamin Disraeli (1804–1881)**, who served respectively in 1868 and from 1874 to 1880. Victoria fully endorsed Disraeli's plan to protect British foreign interests and to strengthen and increase the British Empire. In 1876, he had her crowned **Empress of India**. Conversely, she was continually at odds with the Liberal **William Gladstone (1809–1898)**, who served as prime minister four times between 1868 and 1894, because he favored reforms such as legalizing trade unions and Irish Home Rule.

During the **Crimean War (1853–1856)**, Victoria instituted the **Victoria Cross** for bravery and actively supported the pioneering work of nurse **Florence Nightingale** (see no. 46). By the time she celebrated her diamond jubilee, or sixtieth anniversary of ascending the crown, in 1897, her popularity had reached its height both at home and abroad. She died in Osborne at the age of eighty-two and was buried beside Albert near Windsor.

◆ A liberal Quaker and radical reformer, women's rights activist—known in her time as a suffragist—**SUSAN BROWNELL ANTHONY** devoted fifty years of her life to secure the right of American women to vote. As she stated in an 1873 address: "It was we the people, not we the white male citizens, nor yet we, the male citizens, but we, the whole people, who formed the Union."

Born in Adams, Massachusetts, the second of eight children, Anthony began teaching school at age fifteen, a career she continued for fifteen years. She was strongly opposed to the use of liquor and took part in the temperance movement between 1848 and 1853, founding the first temperance society in America in New York in 1852. One of her greatest achievements was her ability to rally vast numbers of people of both sexes around a single goal. From 1856 to 1861 she used this talent in her work for the **Anti-Slavery Society**. During the **American Civil War (1861–1865)**, she established the **Women's National Loyal League** to work for the emancipation of slaves.

In 1851, **Elizabeth Cady Stanton** (see no. 38) recruited Anthony for the women's suffrage movement. Between 1854 and 1860, they concentrated their efforts on reforming New York State's discriminatory laws. Convinced that true reforms would not occur until women had the right to vote, they founded the **American Woman Suffrage Association** in 1869 to work toward the passage of a constitutional amendment. Between 1858 and 1860, they published a weekly newspaper called *Revolution*, whose motto was "The true republic—men, their rights and nothing more; women, their rights and nothing less." In 1872, asserting that the Fifteenth Amendment to the Constitution entitled her to do so, Anthony cast a ballot in the presidential election. She was arrested and fined $100, but she defiantly refused to pay.

After meeting with activists in Europe, Anthony and Stanton helped form the **International Council of Women** in 1888 with representatives from forty-eight countries. She continued speaking at conventions until her death in Rochester, New York, at the age of eighty-six.

In 1878, **Senator A. A. Sargent** introduced a women's suffrage amendment known as the **Susan B. Anthony Amendment**, which languished for forty-two years before being ratified as the **Nineteenth Amendment** on August 26, 1920. On July 2, 1979, in honor of her achievements, the U.S. government issued the Susan B. Anthony dollar coin, making her the first American woman to have her picture on a circulated coin.

Considered to be the founder of modern nursing, British nurse, hospital reformer, and public health innovator **FLORENCE NIGHTINGALE** was born in Florence, Italy, and raised in the countryside of Derbyshire, England. Believing she had a calling from God, she decided to dedicate her life to nursing. After traveling through Europe in 1849 to study hospital systems, she trained at the Institute of Saint Vincent de Paul in Alexandria, Egypt, and the Institute for Protestant Deaconesses in Kaiserswerth, Germany. In 1853, she used her allowance to reorganize the **Institution for the Care of Sick Gentlewomen** on Harley Street in London, gaining valuable experience in hospital administration.

In 1853, Russia invaded Turkey and ignited the **Crimean War (1853–1856)**. Aware of Nightingale's success on Harley Street, Britain's **Secretary of War Sidney Herbert** asked her to undertake a nursing mission in the Crimea. She and thirty-eight nurses went to Üsküdar (now part of Istanbul), where they found 5,000 British soldiers housed in filthy, dilapidated buildings that not only lacked medical equipment but even the barest living essentials. Under Nightingale's direction, the nurses cleaned and disinfected the vermin-filled barracks. Each night, by the light of a lantern she carried, the "Lady with the Lamp" ended her twenty-hour workday by personally inspecting every ward. Within months, casualties from infection dropped from 42 percent to 2.2 percent.

After the war, Nightingale returned to England as a national heroine. In 1857, encouraged by **Queen Victoria** (see no. 44), Nightingale began the first scientific examination of the sanitary conditions and health of the peacetime army. Her book *Notes on Matters Affecting the Health, Efficiency and*

Hospital Administration of the British Army remains the standard work of its kind. She gradually widened the scope of her work to include civilian hospitals and public health.

In 1860, with money raised through donations, Nightingale founded the **Nightingale School of Nursing** at St. Thomas' Hospital, the first professional nursing program in the world. Prior to this time, nursing was considered a menial job undertaken by untrained personnel who were often of dubious character. By establishing strict standards, Nightingale raised nursing to the level of a medical profession. She outlined her methods in *Notes on Nursing* (1859), the first textbook for nurses.

In 1907, Nightingale became the first woman to receive the British **Order of Merit**. After her death, the **Guards Crimean War Memorial** was erected in her honor on Waterloo Place in London in 1915.

Born **Araminta Ross** in 1820 near Cambridge, Maryland, one of eleven children of **Benjamin and Harriet (Green) Ross**, **HARRIET TUBMAN** took her mother's first name. At age thirteen, she was seriously wounded by a two-pound weight when she inserted herself between a fleeing slave and an overseer. During her recovery, she began to question the workings of a society in which she had no power.

In 1844, she married **John Tubman**, a free black man, but when she escaped to the North in 1849, he remained behind. In Philadelphia, she supported herself by working as a cook and a domestic worker, and after saving enough money, she traveled back to the South and led her sister **Mary Ann Bowley** and her two children to freedom. By 1857, she had freed her entire family.

Carrying a long rifle—to encourage fleeing slaves who had second thoughts as well as to defend against attack—Tubman made nineteen trips, leading an estimated 300 people to freedom in Canada along an "underground" network of "safe houses" that became known as the **Underground Railroad**. She became so notorious that rewards for her capture totaled $40,000. She was financially supported in her work by many leading activists of the day. One ally, **William Still** of the **Vigilance Committee of Philadelphia**, an abolitionist group, wrote of her: "...[in] point of courage, shrewdness and disinterested exertions to rescue her fellow man, she was without equal." To her own people, however, Tubman was known as **Moses**, for like the biblical character, she led them out of slavery to a better life.

Although historically Tubman is best remembered for her work on the Underground Railroad, she was also a nurse, a spy, and an outspoken feminist reformer.

During the **American Civil War (1861–1865)**, she tended wounded soldiers and helped newly freed slaves learn self-sufficiency. On one occasion, the U.S. War Department directed her to organize a group of eight black men to scout the inland waterways of South Carolina in advance of the troops of Union General Richard Montgomery. Later she personally assisted General Montgomery during a raid.

After the war, Tubman moved to Auburn, New York, where she opened the **Harriet Tubman Home** for the aged and raised funds for schools for former slaves. She also enjoyed a longtime friendship with pioneer suffragist **Susan Brownell Anthony** (see no. 45), with whom she was active in the **New England Anti-Slavery Society** and the **New England Woman Suffrage Association**. In 1896, she was a speaker at the first annual convention of the **National Federation of Afro-American Women**. After a two-year residence in her retirement home, she died of pneumonia at the age of ninety-three.

◆ Known as the **"angel of the battlefield"** during the **American Civil War (1861–1865)**, nurse and philanthropist **CLARA BARTON** was the founder of the **American Association of the Red Cross (now American Red Cross)**. Born in Oxford, Massachusetts, she established several free schools in New Jersey, and during the Civil War she organized her own volunteers to distribute supplies to battlefields, even driving a four-mule wagon team herself. After the war, she set up a bureau of records in Washington, DC, to search for missing soldiers and identified and marked 12,000 graves at the Andersonville National Cemetery in Georgia.

Between 1869 and 1873, Barton lived in Europe, where she founded military hospitals during the **Franco-German War (1870-1871)**, for which she was decorated with the Iron Cross by the German emperor. She also became acquainted with the work of the **International Red Cross**, which was started by Swiss citizen **Henry Dunant**, co-recipient of the first **Nobel Peace Prize** in 1901.

In 1881, Barton organized the American Red Cross according to the **Geneva Convention of 1863**, which also set up guidelines for the international organization, and served as president until 1904. Between 1884 and 1903, she represented the United States at the international convention four times and authored the "American amendment" to the Constitution of the Red Cross, which provided services in peacetime as well as in war. The **American Red Cross** was officially chartered in 1901 and again in 1905—a charter that is still in force today.

Barton personally supervised Red Cross relief services during the yellow fever epidemic in Florida (1887), the infamous Johnstown (Pennsylvania) flood (1889), the Russian famine (1891), the Hamidian massacres (1894–1896), the **Spanish-American War (1898)**, and the **South African War (1899–1902)**.

Barton's books include *An Official History of the Red Cross* (1882), *The Red Cross in Peace and War* (1898), and her autobiography, *The Story of My Childhood* (1907). She died in Glen Echo, Maryland, at the age of ninety-one.

Today, worldwide Red Cross services are organized into the following programs: 1) services for armed forces personnel and their families; 2) disaster relief and preparedness; 3) a blood donation program (the largest in the world); 4) nursing and health assistance; 5) safety and first aid training; 6) youth leadership training; and 7) liaison work with the International Red Cross. Every year, more than one million volunteers are active in Red Cross work in America.

ELIZABETH BLACKWELL, the first woman medical doctor in the United States, was born in Counterslip, Bristol, England, one of twelve children in a family of advocates of social reform. Her famous sisters-in-law included **Antoinette Brown Blackwell (1825–1921)**, the first ordained woman minister in America, and women's rights activist **Lucy Stone** (see no. 42). In 1832, after a fire destroyed her father's refinery, the family emigrated to New York, where all the Blackwells became involved in the anti-slavery movement, offering their home as a haven for enslaved persons escaping to the North.

When Blackwell was seventeen, her family moved to Cincinnati, Ohio, and her father died soon after. To support their mother and nine surviving children, the women operated a boarding school for four years. However, being a schoolteacher did not appeal to Blackwell. More as an expression of her resentment of social inequalities than from a passion for medicine, Blackwell decided to become a physician. As she stated in her autobiography from 1895, "The idea of winning a doctor's degree gradually assumed the aspect of a great moral struggle."

Rebuffed by numerous schools including Harvard and Yale, Blackwell entered New York's Geneva Medical College, graduating first in her class in 1849. Her first practical experience occurred in 1848 when she helped to combat a typhoid epidemic. She later wrote her thesis on this subject. After receiving her degree, she studied at St. Bartholomew's Hospital in London and around Continental Europe, returning to New York in 1851. Ostracized in her attempts to set up a medical practice, Blackwell and her sister **Emily Blackwell**, also a physician, bought a house in a slum area with the aid of Quaker friends and opened the **New York**

Infirmary for Indigent Women and Children (later called the **New York Infirmary**). From its inception, the Infirmary always had an entirely female staff, the first such institution ever founded. A medical college was added in 1868, and **Sophia Louisa Jex-Blake** (see no. 54) was the first student to register.

Leaving the operation of the Infirmary to her sister Emily, she returned to England in 1869, where she became one of the founders of the **National Health Society**. In 1874, jointly with Jex-Blake, Blackwell founded the London School of Medicine for Women, where she was a professor of gynecology from 1875 to 1907. Her writings include *The Physical Education of Girls* (1852) and her autobiography *Pioneer Work in Opening the Medical Profession to Women* (1895). She died in Hastings, England, at the age of eighty-nine.

As the founder of the **Church of Christ, Scientist (Christian Science), MARY BAKER EDDY** developed a system of religious philosophy so unique that even today it is seen as being outside the mainstream of traditional Christian belief. Born near Concord, New Hampshire, Eddy was a sickly child who had to be tutored at home. Even after the birth of her only child in 1843, her continuing poor health kept her confined to her home where she ran a school.

Eddy's interest in religious healing first surfaced when she was twelve. As she lay sick with a fever, her mother exhorted her to pray. "I prayed, and a soft glow...[c]ame over me," she reported later. "The fever was gone." In 1862, still suffering from chronic illness, she consulted **Phineas Parkhurst Quimby**, a spiritual healer. Finding relief after he prayed with her, she adopted his philosophy that disease could be cured by spiritual concentration.

However, her discovery of Christian Science resulted from an accident that occurred in 1866. Eddy slipped on an icy street and severely injured herself. On the third day of her convalescence, it is said that she read an account in Matthew 9:2 and experienced an immediate recovery: "Some men brought to him a paralyzed man, lying on a mat. When Jesus saw their faith, he said to the man, 'Take heart, son; your sins are forgiven.'"

After this, Eddy regarded the Bible as a "textbook" that could make her understand the nature of her healing. As she wrote in the main study text for her new religion, *Science and Health with Key to the Scriptures* (1879), "I apprehended for the first time, in their spiritual meaning, Jesus' teaching... [a]nd the principle and rule of spiritual Science and metaphysical healing, in a word, Christian Science." Eddy also wrote a dozen other religious works, including her autobiography, *Retrospection and Introspection*.

Eddy's thinking appealed to many, especially women, who found little relief in medical science. After she founded the **Christian Science Association** in 1875, she became the first practitioner and teacher of her philosophy, supervising every phase of the growing Christian Science movement. In 1881, she opened the **Massachusetts Metaphysical College** to train other practitioners, or mental healers, charging $300 for a course of study. The **First Church of Christ, Scientist** was opened in Boston, Massachusetts, in 1894. In that same year, she founded the **Christian Science Publishing Society**, and in 1908, the *Christian Science Monitor* published for the first time. When she died at her home near Boston at the age of 89, she left an estate worth $2.5 million.

Clad in a black bonnet and dress with a lace collar, one woman became a familiar sight to striking workers across America during the late nineteenth and early twentieth centuries. Called **MOTHER JONES** by those she organized to strike for better wages and working conditions, **Mary Harris** was born in Cork, Ireland, and emigrated to Canada when she was five. In 1861, she married ironworker and unionist **George Jones**, who along with their four children died during the 1867 yellow fever epidemic. After the **Great Chicago Fire of 1871** destroyed all her possessions, she became involved in labor organizing.

In 1877, Jones joined the striking workers of the **Baltimore and Ohio Railroad (B&O)** and watched as they set fire to 100 freight cars, causing five million dollars in damages. In the early 1880s, she became a fiery orator for **United Mine Workers**, and became known as "Mother," crisscrossing the country to rally support with her slogan "Join the union, boys." In 1898 she was a founding member of the **Social Democratic Party**.

Mine owners often hired "scabs" to replace striking workers. In Arnot, Pennsylvania, Jones organized a brigade of miners' wives to wait outside the mine. When mule-drawn carts brought the scabs out, the women began screaming and banging dishpans, and the animals bolted in fear. Another time, when her brigade was jailed, Jones instructed them to sing continuously in their cells. After five days, they were released.

By 1905, three-quarters of all miners belonged to the union. That same year, Jones was the only woman invited to attend the founding meeting of the **Industrial Workers of the World (IWW)**, or **Wobblies**. After a West Virginia strike in 1912, she was sentenced to 20 years' imprisonment for conspiracy, but was reprieved by the governor. When she was jailed following a march in Denver, Colorado, a workers' revolt on her behalf resulted in the 1914 **Ludlow Massacre**, where National Guard troops killed 13 women and children. By publicizing this atrocity nationwide, she was able to galvanize public opinion in the miners' favor.

Jones was also a strong advocate of legislation to prohibit child labor, and in 1903, she headed a march of child laborers from their Pennsylvania textile plant to the home of **President Theodore Roosevelt (1858–1919)** in New York so "he could hear the wail of children who never had a chance to go to school." A state law was subsequently passed that barred children under 14 from performing factory work.

Between 1915 and 1919, Jones supported garment worker strikes in New York and Chicago and numerous streetcar strikes nationwide before joining the Great Steel Strike of 1919. In 1921, at the age of ninety-one, she attended a meeting of the **Pan-American Federation of Labor** in Mexico, where she got a resolution passed to free all political prisoners. When she died at the age of one hundred, she was buried near the graves of strike victims in the Union Miners Cemetery of southern Illinois.

Although her father, philosopher and visionary educator **Amos Bronson Alcott (1799–1888)** promoted revolutionary teaching methods that inspired ridicule and brought financial ruin to his family, **LOUISA MAY ALCOTT**, who was born in Germantown (later part of Philadelphia), Pennsylvania, and raised in Boston, Massachusetts, enjoyed a happy childhood with her four sisters. She was tutored by author **Ralph Waldo Emerson (1803–1882)**, a close family friend, and writer **Henry David Thoreau (1817–1862)**. Jurist **Oliver Wendell Holmes (1841–1935)** and writer **Nathaniel Hawthorne (1804–1864)** often visited her home. Her backyard playhouse included diaries and dictionaries, which she learned how to use before she was five years old. In this atmosphere, she developed strong opinions on politics and social reform.

To help with family finances, Alcott worked various jobs, including making doll dresses, teaching, and domestic service. At that time, wild and sensational stories, known as **potboilers**, could earn five or ten dollars, so she tried her hand at writing stories with titles like *Whispers in the Dark*, which were later published in her collected works. Her first book, *Flower Fables* (1854), was a collection of tales originally written for Emerson's daughter, Ellen.

During the **American Civil War (1861–1865)**, Alcott volunteered as a nurse in Washington, DC, supporting herself as a seamstress and governess. The letters she wrote to her family during this period were published as *Hospital Sketches*, first as a serial in *Commonwealth* magazine and then as a book in 1863, and established her reputation as a writer. In 1868, she became editor of a magazine for children called *Merry's Museum*.

Alcott's most famous work, *Little Women* (1868), an autobiographical novel about her childhood, which depicts warm and funny family relationships, is one of the most enduringly popular children's books ever written. It sold 87,000 copies within three years. This book and its sequel, *Little Men* (1871), which introduced readers to fictionalized versions of her nephews, are considered children's classics. Her other works include *Moods* (1864), *An Old-Fashioned Girl* (1870), *Work* (1873), *Spinning Wheel Stories* (1884), *Jo's Boys* (1886), and numerous short stories and sketches.

Alcott was also active in the causes of abolition and women's suffrage. She died in Boston in 1888 at the age of fifty-five.

◆ **LAKSHMI BAI** became a national Indian heroine when she died for justice while leading troops during the **Indian Mutiny (1857–1858)**. Born in India as **Manikarnika** (a name for a sacred place on the Ganges River), the daughter of a Brahman official, she grew up with her brothers and her father, who taught her martial arts and how to ride a horse.

Upon her marriage to Maharaja **Gangadhar Rao** of Jhansi, she changed her name to **Lakshmi**, the Hindu goddess of wealth and good fortune. When she and her husband were unable to have a son, they adopted his cousin. After Gangadhar died in 1853, the governor-general, the **marquess of Dalhousie**, announced that since there was no heir—adoption did not count—the colonial British government planned to annex Jhansi. This decision flew in the face of Hindu beliefs that an adopted son was equally capable of performing the ritual sacrifices necessary to spare his father the fires of hell.

Indian historians later cited Dalhousie's annexation policy as one of the main causes of the Indian Mutiny, also known as the **Sepoy Mutiny**. (Sepoys were native troops serving in non-Indian armies.) Another causal factor was the fact that Westernization threatened to overthrow the existing caste system and undermine the authority of the Brahmans (orthodox Hindus of the highest caste).

Rani, or queen, Lakshmi sent two petitions to appeal Dalhousie's decision. When he turned them down in February 1854, she hired a British counsel and appealed to London. That appeal was also refused, and she then retired from public view for three years.

By 1857, the Mutiny was well underway, and on July 7, the sepoys massacred British civilians at **Star Fort**. Although Lakshmi was forced under threat of death to give the rebels money and elephants, the British believed that she was involved in the massacre. Thus, in March 1858, the British laid siege to the city of Jhansi. Lakshmi, who remained constantly visible to both her troops and the enemy throughout the battle, was able to escape shortly before the city fell. Lakshmi rode to the city of Kalpi, where she was given a heroine's welcome. Putting on armor and a sword with a jeweled scabbard, she led her troops on a successful mission to recapture the neighboring fortress of Gwalior. However, when British reinforcements attacked, she was killed during hand-to-hand combat while defending the city of Morar.

Statues in honor of Rani Lakshmi Bai have been erected in Jhansi and **Gwalior**, and her memory has been preserved in numerous folk ballads such as this one: "The song of joy, the song of freedom rises/In every corner of the land this song is heard/Here fought Lakshmi Bai..." During the nationalist movement in the twentieth century that culminated in India's independence in 1947, the rani of Jhansi became an inspirational symbol of Indian bravery and patriotism.

◆ A committed and forceful advocate of a woman's right to practice medicine in the British Isles, **SOPHIA LOUISA JEX-BLAKE** became the first woman medical doctor in Scotland. She was born in Hastings, England, the youngest daughter of a proctor of Doctors' Commons, and in 1858, she entered Queen's College in London, where she was a tutor in mathematics while pursuing her degree. When she was 25, she sailed to Boston to observe American teaching methods. She recorded her impressions in *A Visit to Some American Schools and Colleges* (1867).

Jex-Blake became interested in medicine as a "cause worth fighting for and a field of service that should be open to all women" and applied to Harvard and other medical schools. When she was turned away, she became the first student to enroll at the Woman's Medical College of the New York Infirmary founded by **Elizabeth Blackwell** (see no. 49). However, after only a year, her studies were postponed due to her father's death. In 1869, after the University of London refused to admit her, she and four other women, following a strenuous campaign, were allowed to enroll at the University of Edinburgh. However, they were refused permission to study at the Royal Infirmary, a necessary step to completing a degree. When the women tried to enter the Infirmary, male students blocked their way, and a riot ensued. This incident—plus the fact that, although a woman had placed first in the Hope Scholarship exam, a man was awarded the prize—aroused public sentiment in the women's favor. Officials then declared that women could only receive "certificates of proficiency" not diplomas. The women filed a lawsuit, and three years later in 1876, the **Russell Gurney Enabling Act** allowed women to be tested for graduation.

Meanwhile, in 1874, Jex-Blake and Elizabeth Blackwell founded the **London School of Medicine for Women**. In 1877, Jex-Blake graduated with a medical degree from the University of Berne and practiced medicine in England. The following year she returned to Edinburgh, where she opened a dispensary, which in 1885, became the **Edinburgh Hospital and Dispensary for Women and Children**, making her the first woman doctor in Scotland. In 1886, she organized the **Edinburgh School of Medicine for Women**. In 1894, largely through her influence, the University of Edinburgh accorded women students full rights, and she subsequently closed her school because it was no longer needed. She chronicled her and other women's experiences in *Medical Women* (1886). She died in Sussex, England, at the age of seventy-one.

Fellow **Fabian Society** member and dramatist **George Bernard Shaw (1856–1950)** once described social activist **ANNIE BESANT** as "a sort of expeditionary force [whose] displays of personal courage and resolution [compelled people] to listen by sheer force of style and character." These qualities of character would lead Besant into a reform career that spanned fifty years and two continents.

Born in London, Besant became involved in socialist causes that included publishing a pamphlet advocating birth control, for which she was brought to trial on a charge of obscenity. In 1885, she joined the Fabian Society, a group founded in 1884 to work for social change through legislative means, through which she became known as a gifted orator. As a journalist, she became aware of the plight of blue-collar workers, many of whom were jobless due to a decade-long economic depression. On November 13, 1887, known as **Bloody Sunday**, she took part in a workers' march, which was dispersed by police on horseback wielding truncheons, an experience which intensified her commitment to fight poverty and oppression.

"Match girls" at the **Bryant and May factory** in the East End of London made matches while standing at benches for up to ten hours a day, under the threat of heavy fines for mistakes and at risk for **phossy jaw**—a lethal decay of the gums caused by the phosphorus in matches. In June 1888, Besant organized the walkout of 1,400 match girls and whipped up public support in the press by comparing the workers' paltry earnings with the company's hefty profits. After a month-long strike, the women won a generous settlement and formed the seven-hundred-woman **Union of Women Matchmakers**. Their success helped stimulate the growth of other women's unions and also put pressure on male trade unionists to accept women as equals. In the next eight years, the number of women trade unionists grew from 40,000 to 118,000. In 1889, Besant joined the **Theosophical Society** headed by Russian-born spiritualist **Helena Blavatsky (1831–1891)**, who espoused a mystical philosophy based on Indian religious thought. Besant, living in Madras (now Chennai in India), served as president of the Society from 1907 until her death, and she learned Sanskrit and established the **Central Hindu College** in Benares in 1898. After becoming active in the Indian independence movement, in 1916, she founded the **Home Rule League** in India and edited *New India*, a daily paper in Madras. She also served as the fifth president of the **Indian National Congress** in 1917, a unique position for an Englishwoman. Her books include *Autobiography* (1893) and *India, Bond or Free?* (1926). Besant died in Madras, India, at the age of eighty-six.

Born in New York City, the daughter of a wealthy family, poet **EMMA LAZARUS** was surrounded by literature and fine art as a child. One of her books, *Admetus and Other Poems*, was inscribed to her mentor **Ralph Waldo Emerson (1803–1882)** and was published in 1871 when she was twenty-two years old. Her next book was a romance titled *Alide* (1874). She wrote numerous magazine articles and in 1881, *Poems and Ballads of Heinrich Heine*, her translation of Heine's poems from German, was published. Angered by the persecution of Russian Jews in the early 1880s, Lazarus became an ardent Zionist, and in 1882, published *Songs of a Semite*, which was a militant call to arms. This collection of works included her translations of medieval Jewish poems and a religious piece, "The Dance of Death," based on an accusation that Jews had caused Europe's **Black Death** in the **Middle Ages** by poisoning well water.

Lazarus is most well remembered for her sonnet "The New Colossus" (1883), which she donated to an auction to raise money for the **Statue of Liberty** fund. The poem was then inscribed on a tablet near the base of the statue. Unveiled on October 28, 1886, the statue, located on **Liberty Island** (formerly **Bedloe's Island**) at the entrance to New York Harbor, is that of a woman in a flowing robe wearing a spiked crown and holding a lit torch aloft with her right arm and clutching a book in her left, which is engraved with the words "July 4, 1776."

The Statue of Liberty is made of copper and iron, and together the statue and its pedestal stand over 305 feet from the ground, making it one of the tallest such monuments in the world. A gift from the government of France as a gesture of international friendship to the United States, the Statue of Liberty has become the most well-known symbol of freedom in the world. Between 1892 and 1954, over twelve million immigrants were filled with hope at the sight of the statue, which greeted them on their way to **Ellis Island**.

Lazarus died in New York City in 1887 at the age of thirty-eight, but her legacy on the Statue of Liberty lives on, expressing her ardent belief that the United States was a safe haven for the oppressed. The last and most famous lines of her poem are:

Give me your tired, your poor,
Your huddled masses yearning to
*   breathe free,*
The wretched refuse of your teeming
*   shore.*
Send these, the homeless, tempest-tost
*   to me,*
I lift my lamp beside the golden door!

EMMELINE PANKHURST, the matriarch of Britain's most militant family of women's rights activists, was born in Manchester and attended her first suffrage meeting with her mother at the age of fourteen. In 1879, she married **Richard Pankhurst**, a barrister who drafted Britain's first women's suffrage bill and later the **Married Women's Property Act of 1882** for political economist **John Stuart Mill (1806–1873)**. After Richard died in 1898, leaving her with four children, she became the Registrar in Rushholme, a working-class district of Manchester. Observing the legal and social oppression of women, she decided that only equal political rights could emancipate women and reform society. In 1903, Emmeline became disillusioned with the **Independent Labor Party's (ILP)** lack of progress toward securing women's suffrage and formed her own organization, the **Women's Social and Political Union (WSPU)**, with her three daughters **Christabel (1880–1958)**, **Sylvia (1882–1960)**, and **Adela (1885–1961)** under the slogan "Votes for Women."

Christabel attended school in Manchester and Switzerland. In 1901, while studying law at Victoria University, she became a member of the **North of England Society for Women's Suffrage** and the **Manchester Women's Trade Union Council**. In 1905, after two years of active campaigning, she along with mill worker **Annie Kenney (1879–1953)** were arrested for protesting at a Liberal Party meeting in 1905. Offered a small fine or jail, the women chose jail, an action which catapulted the WSPU into national prominence.

Meanwhile, Emmeline moved to London to live with Sylvia, an artist. Sylvia later founded WSPU branches in the East End of London between 1912 and 1913, from which she eventually formed a separate organization, the **East London Federation of the**

EMMELINE PANKHURST

Suffragettes. In 1935, she published *The Life of Emmeline Pankhurst*. Adela, though initially involved with the WSPU, emigrated to Australia, where she helped organize the **Victorian Socialist Party** and was active in the right wing **Australia First Movement**.

Christabel joined her mother in London in 1907, and for the next six years, she was the WSPU's chief organizer and orator. The WSPU's mass marches to the Houses of Parliament and disruption of official meetings brought an immediate response from police, and the ensuing newspaper coverage quickly spread their message across Britain. By 1908, frustrated by Prime Minister **Herbert Asquith**'s continued resistance and delaying tactics in Parliament, Emmeline and Christabel adopted more radical protest measures. They smashed windows in London's shopping district, burned letters in mailboxes, wrote "Votes for Women" in acid on golf course greens, chained themselves to gates outside the homes of government officials, defaced paintings, and even burned an unoccupied building. However, their tactics were always aimed at property only and never endangered human lives.

Emmeline was arrested for the first time in 1908. Like other WSPU members, she chose jail over a fine and then went on a hunger strike. By the time of her conviction in 1913 for incitement to violence (for which she received a three-year sentence), the government had passed the **Prisoners Temporary Discharge for Ill Health Act**. Popularly known as the **Cat and Mouse Act**, it allowed hunger-striking prisoners to be temporarily released until they regained their strength. Rearrested twelve more times, Emmeline was reduced to such a state of weakness that after only a day or two on a hunger strike, the government was forced to release her as they could not risk her dying in custody.

In 1912, threatened with a conspiracy charge, Christabel fled to Paris, where she continued to direct WSPU strategy and publish *The Suffragette*. Her series of articles for this newspaper on venereal disease, which by the standards of the time were quite outspoken, were later published as a book, *The Great Scourge*. During **World War I (1914–1918)**, this book was reprinted as a guide for soldiers. Christabel eventually settled in California in 1940. Her last book, *Unshackled: The Story of How We Won the Vote*, was published in 1959.

The WSPU continued its militant campaign for women's suffrage until the outbreak of World War I in 1914, when its members redirected their energies toward the war effort.

That same year, Emmeline's autobiography, *My Own Story*, was published. She died in London in 1928, just one month before passage of the **Representation of the People Act** that granted full voting rights

CHRISTABEL PANKHURST

to all English women. Subsequently, in 1929 trade union leader **Margaret Bondfield (1873–1953)** became the first woman cabinet member in British history. Today, a statue of Emmeline stands in the Victoria Tower Gardens near the Houses of Parliament in London.

Born **Carrie Lane** in Ripon, Wisconsin, women's rights activist **CARRIE CHAPMAN CATT** graduated from Iowa State College (now a university) and then worked as a teacher and principal in the schools of Madison City, Iowa, and as a journalist in San Francisco, California. After her husband **Leo Chapman** died, she returned to Iowa and married **George Catt**, an engineer, in 1890. In that same year, she began working on a suffrage campaign with **Susan B. Anthony (1820–1906) (see no. 45)** in South Dakota.

Known as an excellent administrator, Catt first served as chairperson of the **Organization Committee of the National American Woman Suffrage Association (NAWSA)** from 1895 to 1899, whereafter she succeeded Anthony as president from 1900 to 1904. She was re-elected president in 1915, holding this post for thirty-two years until her death. In 1904, she helped organize the **International Woman Suffrage Alliance**, which held its first meeting in Berlin that year, and she served as its president from 1904 to 1923.

Between 1909 and 1915, Catt structured **NAWSA** along political district lines, so that while working for the vote, women could receive training in political action techniques. Due largely in part to Catt's ability to mobilize association members into an effective lobbying force, suffrage was granted in the states of Colorado (1893); Utah and Idaho (1896); Washington (1910); California (1911); Kansas, Oregon, and Arizona (1912); Nevada and Montana (1914); and New York (1917). In 1920, women's suffrage was granted nationwide when the **Nineteenth Amendment** to the U.S. Constitution was ratified, which provided that "The right of citizens of the United States to vote shall not be denied or abridged by the United States or any state on account of sex." Later that year,

Catt reorganized **NAWSA**, a two-million-member organization, as the **National League of Women Voters**.

In 1925, Catt brought together eleven national women's organizations to form the **National Committee on the Cause and Cure of War**, serving as president from 1925 to 1932. The purpose of this organization was to educate the American public about the United States' participation in world peace organizations. After **World War II (1939–1945)**, her interest in world peace extended to the **United Nations**, where she used her influence to have qualified women named to various commissions.

◆ An exceptional writer, tireless social activist, committed worker for peace, champion of civil rights, social work pioneer, and feminist, **JANE ADDAMS** was one of the most influential women in American history. Born the eighth of nine children to a prosperous banker and miller in Cedarville, Illinois, she was deeply influenced by her family's abolitionist convictions and Quaker faith. In 1882, she graduated in the first class at the Rockford Seminary.

In 1889, Addams and **Ellen Starr (1859–1940)** opened **Hull House**, the first settlement house in the United States. Located on Halstead Street in the heart of a factory district in Chicago, Illinois, Hull House was staffed by Addams' college-educated contemporaries, who provided a wide range of social services, including food, clothing, and medical care, and leisure time activities. Hull House quickly became a gathering place for people of all ages from the diverse surrounding community of mostly non-English-speaking immigrants. In the wake of the **Industrial Revolution**, Addams became a recognized leader in organized efforts to solve the social welfare needs of America's teeming cities. Many of her ideas were later incorporated into the **New Deal** policies of **President Franklin D. Roosevelt (1882–1945)**.

In 1912, Addams played a prominent role in founding the **National Progressive Party** and organized the **Women's Peace Party**, serving as its chairperson in 1915. That same year, she was elected president of the **International Congress of Women** at its meeting in The Hague and president of the **Women's International League for Peace and Freedom**, serving as a delegate to congresses in Europe and the United States between 1919 and 1929. In 1920, she became one of the founders of the **American Civil Liberties Union (ACLU)**.

Her opposition to entering **World War I** caused her expulsion from the **Daughters of the American Revolution (DAR)**, who called her "the most dangerous woman in America today." However, Addams' strong peace stance was vindicated when **President Woodrow Wilson (1856–1924)** based his recommendations for postwar peace on her proposals. For her efforts, she shared the **1931 Nobel Peace Prize** with educator **Nicholas Murray Butler (1862–1947)**.

Her books include: *Democracy and Social Ethics* (1902), *Newer Ideals of Peace* (1907), *The Spirit of Youth and the City Streets* (1909), *Twenty Years at Hull House* (1910), *A New Conscience and an Ancient Evil* (1911), *The Long Road of Woman's Memory* (1916), *Peace and Bread in Time of War* (1922), *The Second Twenty Years at Hull-House* (1930), and *The Excellent Becomes the Permanent* (1932).

◆ Explorer **MARY KINGSLEY** was born in London, England, the daughter of a wealthy doctor who traveled frequently to pursue studies in anthropology and natural history. Her only formal education was in German, which her father saw as useful for conducting research on his behalf. In 1892, after serving as her mother's nursemaid for fifteen years, her parents died, and her brother moved away. Left on her own for the first time, Kingsley, then twenty-nine, took a holiday to the Canary Islands where tales of Africa inspired her to continue her father's work.

In August 1893, Kingsley sailed from Liverpool aboard the *Lagos*, a small cargo ship, on the first of several trips to Africa. She had made an arrangement with the **British Museum** to collect specimens of river fish, and she brought back sixty-five species, many previously unknown, three of which the museum named in her honor.

Kingsley based her expedition on trade, which not only gave her access to remote African tribes but also made her financially independent. She deplored the European influence in Africa, particularly that of missionaries, who viewed natives as savages that needed to be "educated" rather than as people with unique cultures that were worthy of respect. In her perspective, traders were more honorable, providing business opportunities for Africans without trying to recast their complex cultures into a European mold.

Exploring the Calabar and Ogowe rivers in the former Belgian Congo, she mixed freely with the **Fang**, a tribe that cultivated the image of a cannibalistic people, earning their respect by trading tobacco, pocketknives, and colorful handkerchiefs in a forthright manner. As she described it in *Travels in West Africa* (1897): "A certain sort of friendship arose... We each recognized that we belonged to that same section of the human race with whom it is better to drink than to fight." An intrepid adventurer, she survived a fall into a spiked game pit, waded across leech-filled rivers, and became the second climber to reach the top of Camoron Mountain—the highest point in West Africa. Upon her December 1895 return to England, Kingsley was hailed as a celebrity. Her second book, *West African Studies* (1899), was a powerfully written political tract that indicted the British government's policies in Africa and advocated cooperation between European and African cultures based on mutual respect. A detailed account of her journey can be found in D. Wilcox, *Ten Who Dared* (1977).

During the **South African War** of 1899, Kingsley went to nurse Boer prisoners in Simonstown, Africa, where she contracted typhoid fever and died at the age of thirty-seven. At her request, she was buried at sea.

◆ Physicist **MARIA SKŁODOWSKA** was born in Warsaw, Poland, and received her early training from her father, who was a high school physics teacher. In 1891, she changed her first name to **Marie** and enrolled in the Sorbonne in Paris, where she ranked first in her class when she received her degree in physics. In 1895, she married physicist **Pierre Curie (1859- 1906)**. The Curies' study of **radioactive elements** contributed to an understanding of atoms and helped lay a foundation for modern-day **nuclear physics**.

Following the discovery of **X-rays** by **Wilhelm Roentgen (1845–1923)** in 1895 and **Henri Becquerel's (1852–1908)** discovery that uranium gave off similar invisible radiation in 1896, Marie began to measure the **uranium radiation** in pitchblende, coining the term **radioactive** to describe the elements in the ore that emitted radiation as their nuclei broke down. Her husband Pierre, who had been conducting studies on magnetism, joined Marie in her work. The elements they identified were **radium** and **polonium**, the latter named after Marie's native country of Poland. Beginning in 1898, the Curies used one ton of pitchblende to study radium over a four-year period. In 1903, they shared the **Nobel Prize in Physics** with Henri Becquerel, making Marie the first female Nobel laureate.

After Pierre was killed by a horse-drawn cart in 1906, Marie succeeded him as a professor of physics at the University of Paris, and in 1911, she was awarded an unprecedented second Nobel Prize, this time in chemistry, for her work on **radium compounds**, making her the first person to receive two Nobel Prizes. In 1914, she became head of the Paris Institute of Radium and cofounded the **Curie Institute**. Her published works include *Recherches sur les substances radioactives* (1904) and *Traité de radioactivité* (1910).

Marie Curie's final illness was diagnosed as pernicious anemia, caused by overexposure to radiation. She died in Savoy in France at the age of sixty-six.

The Curies' scientific legacy lived on in their daughter **Irène Joliot-Curie (1897–1956)** who, with her husband **Frédéric Joliot (1900–1958)**, received the **Nobel Prize in Chemistry** in 1935 for the artificial production of radioactive elements.

◆ During the **Reconstruction (1865–1877)** after the **American Civil War (1861–1865)**, though no longer slaves, the lives of African American sharecroppers changed little. Entrepreneur and philanthropist **MADAM C. J. WALKER** was born **Sarah Breedlove** in a windowless shack on a Louisiana plantation. After her parents died, she lived with her older sister, marrying at the age of fourteen to escape her brother-in-law's abuse. In 1885, she had a daughter, **A'Lelia**, but became a widow two years later when her husband was killed by a lynch mob.

Using the traditional "wrap and twist" method to straighten her hair, Walker began to develop bald spots. By experimenting with patent medicines, she developed a formula that not only stopped her hair loss but fostered new growth. Starting with $1.50 worth of ingredients, she and other relatives filled jars with her hair preparation in the attic of her house. She then met and married **C. J. Walker**, a newspaper man who taught her advertising and mail order techniques.

Like most inventors, Walker's preparations were not totally original but improvements on existing products. However, she did invent the **hot comb** and **Wonderful Hair Grower**. She also was the first woman to organize supplies for black hair preparation, develop a steel comb with teeth spaced to comb hair easily, use a mail order system, organize door-to-door agents, and develop her own chain of beauty schools. By 1914, she became the first self-made woman millionaire in the United States. In 1908, Walker founded **Lelia College** in Pittsburgh to train cosmetologists, and in 1913 she opened a second school in New York City. By 1910, Walker had 5,000 sales agents, each averaging $1,000 per day in commissions. By 1919, she had 25,000 agents. Besides selling products, agents taught other women how to set up beauty shops in their homes. Walker strongly promoted the idea of economic self-help, and she believed that if a woman could run a business, she could manage her life.

Walker, who had never attended school, sent A'Lelia to Knoxville College. After building Villa Lewaro, her thirty-four-room mansion on the Hudson River, she hired tutors for herself. An ardent believer in education, she donated money to several Black institutions. She also became a social activist and supported causes that sought to combat racism.

Though a highly successful businesswoman, Walker still had to deal with chauvinism from Black men. Denied an opportunity to speak at the 1912 **National Negro Business League** convention, she pushed her way to the podium and, with great fervor, told the story of her rise from a cotton field in the American South to building her own factory. At the 1913 convention, she served as a presenter on the program.

◆ The daughter of **Sir Hugh Bell**, anthropologist and diplomat **GERTRUDE MARGARET LOWTHIAN BELL** spent her childhood in the countryside of Yorkshire, England, and graduated from Lady Margaret Hall College at Oxford University in 1887. Her archaeological career began with a visit to her uncle, **Sir Frank Lascelles**, then British Minister at Tehran in what is now Iran. Between 1899 and 1914, she made expeditions to the Arabian Peninsula and the Middle East. After these explorations were recorded in works such as *Safar-Nama, Amurath to Amurath, Syria, The Desert and the Sown*, she became an acknowledged authority on the Middle East. She also was known for her translation of Arabic works. Throughout her life, she actively corresponded with a number of people, and in 1927, her letters were published in a two-volume collection titled *The Letters of Gertrude Bell*.

In 1914, when the British assumed control over Iraq at the start of **World War I**, Bell went to work for the British intelligence service collecting information as part of the Arab Bureau. In 1917, she became an assistant to **Sir Percy Cox** in Baghdad, and in this capacity, she became extremely influential in shaping the terms of postwar Iraq's independence from British administration.

In March 1921, **Winston Churchill (1874– 1965)**, then secretary of state for the colonies, organized the **Conference of Cairo** to set up an Arab government in Iraq. At the conference, which was attended by the principal British political and military officials of the Middle East, Bell played a key role in securing the ascension to the throne of King **Faisel I**. On her return to Baghdad, she was instrumental in bringing about the expulsion of Faisel's chief rival. For the next two years, she continued to assist Cox in helping to stabilize the newly installed government.

King Faisel went on to guide Iraq to independence and membership in the League of Nations in 1932.

In 1923, her diplomatic work completed, Gertrude Bell was awarded the post of **Honorary Director of Antiquities** and became the moving force behind the establishment of an archaeological museum in Baghdad. She died there in 1926 at the age of fifty-eight.

A pioneer in industrial toxicology, **ALICE HAMILTON** chose research medicine because she wanted a career that would make her both useful and independent. After receiving her **medical degree** from the University of Michigan in 1893, she studied bacteriology and pathology at the University of Leipzig and the University of Munich in Germany, and also at Johns Hopkins Medical School in Maryland.

In 1897, she became a professor of pathology at Northwestern University, and for the next ten years she lived at **Hull House** founded by **Jane Addams** (see no. 60). Observing conditions in the poverty-stricken factory district, she was outraged that unskilled laborers—most of whom were recent immigrants—were forced by economic necessity to work in conditions that caused disease and death.

After being appointed to the **Illinois Commission on Occupational Diseases**, in 1910, Hamilton became the first American to combine modern laboratory procedures and field research to conduct a survey of industrial poisons. She identified seventy-seven lead-using industries and 578 victims, which led to a groundbreaking state law that required safety measures and physical exams. As a special investigator for the **U.S. Bureau of Labor**, Hamilton crusaded for public health and worker safety. By 1916, she was the leading American authority on lead poisoning and one of only a handful of industrial disease specialists.

In 1919, Harvard University invited Hamilton to become the first woman professor at their medical school (later renamed the School of Public Health) because she was the only person qualified to teach a course in industrial medicine. After **World War I**, her role as a pioneer investigator changed to that of a consultant. A vocal activist and active solicitor of research funds, she was frequently called to testify on such issues as the reform of child labor laws and health insurance. Her book, *Industrial Poisons in the United States* (1925), the first text on the subject, made her one of two worldwide authorities in the field. Between 1924 and 1930, she served on the Health Committee of the **League of Nations** (later becoming the **United Nations**).

In 1935, Department of Labor Chief **Frances Perkins** (see no. 73) hired Hamilton as a consultant in the newly formed **Division of Labor Standards**. It was in this capacity in 1937 that she conducted her last field survey of the viscose rayon industry, which led to the passage of Pennsylvania's first compensation law for an occupational disease.

Hamilton's autobiography, *Exploring the Dangerous Trades*, appeared in 1943. In 1949, a revised version of her 1934 textbook *Industrial Toxicology* was published. Active into her eighties, she died at home of a stroke at the age of 101.

◆ Born in Chiaravalle, Italy, **MARIA MONTESSORI** enrolled in engineering at the University of Rome but graduated with a medical degree in 1894, becoming Italy's first woman doctor. While working at the university's psychiatric unit, she developed a unique educational program that prepared eight-year-old children with mental disabilities to pass the state exam in reading and writing. In 1901, she held the hygiene chair at the **Scuola di Magistero Femminile**, and from 1904 to 1908, she was a professor of anthropology at her alma mater and worked as a government school inspector.

Before beginning her work with other children, Montessori examined educational systems in Europe and found that children were "reduced to immobility" in classrooms, placed in rows like "butterflies transfixed with pins." Such children, she declared, were not "disciplined, but annihilated." As she saw it, the task of the educator was in "seeing that the child does not confound good with immobility and evil with activity." In 1907, she applied her methods to children aged three to six at a **Casa dei Bambini (Children's House)**, a set of rooms set aside for children in the courtyard of tenement buildings in Rome's San Lorenzo slum district. The children, whose parents were illiterate, learned to read, write, and do simple arithmetic. In 1912, Montessori's book *The Montessori Method* described these techniques. Her 1917 book, *Advanced Montessori Method*, detailed her work with children aged six to ten. In contrast to traditional methods, which use a formal process of rewards and punishments, Montessori's method uses a spontaneous learning process and stresses the development of individual initiative and self-reliance by allowing children to move freely and pursue what interests them within a clearly defined framework of acceptable behavior.

Montessori teachers act as guides and supervisors rather than as directors of a set curriculum. They give a child individual instruction and introduce new material as required. When movements are involved, the teacher models them first so a child can learn good habits. The Montessori system also stresses sensory perception and developing motor coordination through activities, games, and simple yet stimulating objects that capture children's interest and promote further exploration.

Montessori spent her later years lecturing and supervising training programs and published *Education for a New World* in 1946. She died in Noordwijk aan Zee in the Netherlands at the age of eighty-one.

◆ One of the most important women in the history of international **socialism**, revolutionary **ROSA LUXEMBURG** was born in Zamość in Russian Poland. As a teenager, she became interested in politics, and upon graduating from the Warsaw Gymnasium, she joined the revolutionary **proletariats**. After fleeing to Switzerland in 1889 to avoid arrest, she earned her doctorate in economics from the University of Zurich with a thesis titled "The Industrial Development of Poland."

In 1893, with **Leo Jogiches**, Luxemburg joined the **Social Democracy of the Kingdom of Poland and Lithuania**. She insisted that workers, rather than seeking Polish independence, should pursue the higher goal of overthrowing the tsar. In 1898, she became a member of the **Social Democratic Party of Germany (SPD)**, the largest and most influential in Europe, and in 1899, she joined the staff of *Vorwärts*, the daily socialist paper. After being imprisoned in 1905, she returned to Poland to organize workers' strikes in Warsaw. Back in Berlin, she began a new career as an instructor of economics at a school for SPD officials (1907–1914) and published her extremely influential pamphlet *The Mass Strike, the Political Party, and the Trade Unions*. She also wrote an economics textbook, and in 1913, she published her most famous work, *The Accumulation of Capital*.

Consistently opposed to nationalism because she believed it destroyed international worker solidarity, Luxemburg was appalled when her fellow socialists supported the war in 1914. She and **Karl Liebknecht (1871–1919)** formed a pacifist faction of the SPD, the **Spartacus League**, and were imprisoned for demonstrating against the war. When she was released in November 1918, she helped transform the Spartacists into the **Communist Party of Germany**.

In her 1922 book *The Russian Revolution*, Luxemburg denounced the excessively centralized structure of **Vladimir Lenin's (1870–1924) Bolsheviks** and the terror that followed the **Russian Revolution**. Instead, she advocated the use of spontaneous, mass political strikes as the main instrument of revolution. In contrast to Lenin, she believed that "the dictatorship of the proletariat consists in the application of democracy not in its abolition."

Arrested in January 1919 for taking part in an unsuccessful Spartacist uprising, she and Liebknecht were then seized by anti-communist German soldiers, who first interrogated and then executed them. Luxemburg's body was thrown into the **Landwehr Canal**. Her murderers were later acquitted.

JULIA MORGAN, whose trailblazing career helped open the field of architecture for American women, was raised in Northern California. In 1890, she became the first woman student at the University of California at Berkeley, College of Engineering. After graduating in 1894, she performed drafting work with **Bernard Maybeck** before becoming the first woman admitted to the Architectural Section of the École des Beaux-Arts in Paris and the first woman to graduate the institution in 1898.

After Morgan became the first woman to receive a state architect's license, **Phoebe Hearst** hired her to remodel her residence in Pleasanton, California, and to collaborate with Maybeck on a family retreat. In the aftermath of the **1906 San Francisco earthquake** and fire, Morgan firmly established her reputation by rebuilding the once-elegant **Fairmont Hotel**. She also designed **St. John's Presbyterian Church**, which became an architectural landmark in Berkeley, and several buildings for **Mills College**, a women's college located in Oakland.

Although Morgan worked in a variety of styles, her favorite was the **Spanish Revival**. Many of her commissions came from women and women's institutions, such as the **Young Women's Christian Association (YWCA)**, for whom she designed buildings in Salt Lake City, Honolulu, and throughout California along with their **Asilomar Conference Center** near Monterey. Although Morgan was not a politically active feminist, she did hire numerous women architects and drafters, and she anonymously provided financial aid to women students.

In 1919, newspaper publisher **William Randolph Hearst (1863–1951)** commissioned Morgan to design a castle retreat on the family ranch at **San Simeon**, midway between San Francisco and Los Angeles, instructing her to incorporate sections of European castles that he had already purchased. She also designed facilities for his offices in San Francisco and Los Angeles and private residences in California and Mexico. These commissions constituted one-third of Morgan's workload for the next twenty years.

Morgan's career reached its height in the late 1920s when she built the **Berkeley City Club** and, with Maybeck, laid out the entire campus of **Principia College** in Elsah, Illinois. In her lifetime, she designed 800 structures.

Acknowledging that she was a decade ahead of most contemporaries in the use of structure as a means of expression, architectural scholars recognize Morgan as one of the prime style innovators of the Western United States during the first half of the twentieth century. She died of a stroke in San Francisco at the age of seventy-five.

◆ The first freeborn member of a slave family of seventeen children from Mayesville, South Carolina, **MARY MCLEOD BETHUNE** went on to become one of the most influential African American women of the twentieth century. During the post-Reconstruction era, few Black people had access to education, but Bethune was able to attend mission schools and become a teacher. Believing that education was the primary route to Black advancement, in 1904 she founded the **Daytona Educational and Industrial Training Institute for Negro Girls** in Daytona Beach, Florida, with "five little girls, a dollar and a half, and faith in God." She conducted the institute in a "head-heart-hand" tradition, offering academic and religious training while having her students work an adjacent farm to provide the school's food.

From the start, the charismatic Bethune forged a bond with both Black and white community leaders and received their financial support. In 1923, she merged her school with the coeducational Cookman Institute to form **Bethune-Cookman College**. In 1943, the college awarded its first degrees in elementary education. This accomplishment made her the first woman of her generation to found an institution for disadvantaged youth that became a four-year college.

This success was the springboard for Bethune's leadership in the Black women's club movement. Through the **National Association of Colored Women (NACW)**, she strove to give Black women an effective voice in public affairs, and she made NACW a vital force in the essentially white **International Council of Women (ICW)**. In 1935, she founded the **National Council of Negro Women (NCNW)**, a lobbying vehicle for social concerns. In 1941, she made NCNW part of the **Women's Interest Section (WIS)** of the War Department, one of the few federally sponsored settings for female leadership. As an assistant to the secretary of war, Bethune ensured that the **Women's Army Auxiliary Corps (WAAC)** allotted ten percent of its officer candidate spaces to Black Americans.

From 1936 to 1944, Bethune was director of Negro Affairs in the **National Youth Administration (NYA)**, a government position higher than that held by any other Black woman in the history of the country up to that time. Enjoying unrestricted access to the White House and close personal relationships with both **President Franklin D. Roosevelt (1882–1971)** and his wife **Eleanor Roosevelt** (see no. 75), she was able to secure federal funding for vocational training and jobs for Black youth, which helped pave the way for Black pilots in the military. Bethune also served as a consultant on interracial affairs at the charter conference of the **United Nations**. She died of a heart attack at the age of eighty.

Birth control pioneer **MARGARET HIGGINS SANGER** was born in Corning, New York, the sixth of eleven children. Watching her mother's endless struggle to raise a large family on a small income and her early death at age forty-nine fueled Sanger's commitment to securing access to reproductive choice for all women. She attended nursing school at White Plains Hospital, and in 1900, she married **William Sanger**, an architect, with whom she had three children in their eight years of marriage.

While working as a midwife and visiting nurse in New York, Sanger became active in the **International Workers of the World's (IWW)** effort to organize textile workers. Following the death of a young client from a self-induced abortion, Sanger focused her efforts on the issue of reproductive autonomy and vowed to establish a nationwide system of advice centers where women could obtain reliable birth control information.

Her militant journal, *The Woman Rebel*, launched in 1914, led to an indictment for violating the postal code. She also distributed a pamphlet called *Family Limitation*, which contained detailed information on birth control techniques. In October 1916, Sanger and her sister **Ethel Byrne** opened a clinic in the Brownsville section of Brooklyn, New York, providing 488 women with contraceptive advice over ten days before the clinic was closed by police. The ensuing trial of the "birth control sisters," which charged Sanger with "maintaining a public nuisance," made her a national figure. She was convicted but won on appeal, opening the way for physicians to give birth control advice in New York City.

In 1921, Sanger founded the **American Birth Control League**, a national lobbying organization, of which she was president until 1928. In 1942, the League became the **Planned Parenthood Federation of America**. In 1927, she organized the first **World Population Conference**. Her **Birth Control Clinical Research Bureau**—the first doctor-staffed clinic in the United States—opened in New York in 1923. The Bureau also served as a teaching facility for doctors. In 1936, Sanger realized one of her life's goals when a federal judge's ruling in the case *United States v. One Package* overturned the notorious **1873 Comstock Act's** classification of birth control as an "obscenity," making it possible for doctors to teach contraception in medical schools. She chronicled her life story in her 1938 book *An Autobiography*.

After **World War II**, Sanger founded the **International Planned Parenthood Federation** and served as its first president. Her efforts also led to the introduction of the first birth control pill in 1960. She died of heart failure in Tucson, Arizona.

A pioneering advocate for the rights of people with disabilities, **HELEN KELLER** was born in Tuscumbia, Alabama. Trapped in a silent, dark world after an illness that left her deaf and blind at the age of nineteen months, she became a willful, destructive child. When she was seven, her family hired **Anne Sullivan (1866–1936)**, a recent graduate of the Perkins Institute for the Blind, as a teacher and governess. After only two weeks, the teacher achieved a breakthrough when her student understood the word "water" that was signed into her hand. After this, a lifelong bond was forged between the two.

In 1900, Keller entered Radcliffe College. Sullivan accompanied her to her classes and signed the lectures into her hand. When the *Ladies' Home Journal* asked Helen to write her autobiography, Sullivan hired Harvard professor John Macy to assist them. Her book, *The Story of My Life*, was published in 1903. In 1904, Helen graduated cum laude, or with distinction. Sullivan and Macy married the following year and remained together until 1913.

In 1906, when New York established its first **State Commission for the Blind**, the governor appointed Keller to it, and she and Macy crisscrossed the country to raise funds. Keller also launched a campaign against ophthalmia neonatorum—blindness in infants—becoming the first person to speak out about how a preventable venereal disease caused this and other devastating illnesses. Later that year, **Mary Agnes Thomson (1885–1960)** joined their household as a live-in housekeeper.

In 1924, the **American Foundation for the Blind (AFB)** made Keller its spokesperson. She also continued to be active in the many social reform movements, including the abolition of child labor and capital punishment. After Macy died in 1936, Thomson became Keller's companion. In the 1930s, Keller effectively lobbied in Washington on behalf of AFB, helping to obtain federally funded reading services and talking books for the blind, and she was instrumental in having the blind included as grant category under Title X of the **Social Security Act**.

During **World War II**, Keller made morale-building tours of military hospitals, and in the 1950s, she gave lecture tours in South Africa, the Middle East, and Latin America on behalf of people with visual impairments. After Thomson's death in 1960, Keller retired from public life. In 1964, she was awarded the **Presidential Medal of Freedom** by **President Lyndon Johnson (1908–1972)**.

Aside from *The Story of My Life* (1903), Keller's books include *The World I Live In* (1908), *Out of the Dark* (1913), *Midstream: My Later Life* (1929), *Let Us Have Faith* (1940), *Teacher: Anne Sullivan Macy* (1955) and *The Open Door* (1957). She also made two documentary films about her life, *Deliverance* (1919) and *Helen Keller in Her Story* (1954).

A pioneer in the use of **physiotherapy** who revolutionized medical treatment for polio patients, **SISTER ELIZABETH KENNY** was born at Kelly's Gully near Warialda in New South Wales, Australia. She first became interested in nursing at the age of fourteen when her frail younger brother sent away for "The Great Sandow's Muscle Course" and she helped drill him in the body-building exercises.

Kenny received only limited formal education as a child, but in her late twenties she decided to study nursing, though she was never certified. When she first began working with patients paralyzed by polio in the Australian bush country in 1911, she was not familiar with the orthodox treatment for the disease, which consisted of immobilizing limbs with casts and splints. Instead, Kenny obtained good results by applying hot blankets and moving, massaging, manipulating, and "re-educating" the muscles. Her methods served to lessen deformity and taught patients how to best use the remaining healthy muscles.

During World War I, she worked as an army transport nurse, tending wounded soldiers on ocean voyages home, which is when she earned the title of "Sister" as nurses in countries in the British Empire were called. After the war, she developed a canopied stretcher on wheels to shuttle patients across the rugged Australian Outback.

In 1933, during one of the frequent polio epidemics, people asked for her help, and Kenny set up a table under an awning in a city called Townsville. News of her success spread quickly. Although conservative doctors criticized her lack of formal education and dismissed her techniques, the governments of New South Wales and Queensland set up a series of "Kenny clinics." In 1940, she traveled to the United States, where she was given an opportunity by the **National Foundation for Infantile Paralysis (NFIP)** (later the **March of Dimes Foundation**) and the University of Minnesota to lecture and demonstrate her methods at the Minneapolis General Hospital. Many doctors, who had become dissatisfied with the results they obtained using traditional methods of immobilizing children in casts and frames, became convinced that Kenny's method did indeed offer a better treatment, particularly in the early stages of the disease.

In 1941, the NFIP's medical advisory committee officially endorsed Kenny's treatment. In 1942, after receiving approval from the **American Medical Association**, the **Elizabeth Kenny Institute** was founded in Minneapolis to train nurses and **physiotherapists** in her techniques. She died in Toowoomba, Queensland, Australia, at the age of sixty-six.

America's first female cabinet member, **FRANCES PERKINS** is remembered as a champion of the nation's working class. Born in Boston, Massachusetts, she attended Mount Holyoke College then taught for several years before receiving her master of arts in social economics at Columbia University in 1910. While living in Chicago, she worked at the **Hull House**, where she had her first experience with labor unions when she helped workers collect back wages.

As secretary of the **Consumers' League of New York** from 1910 to 1912, Perkins drew attention to sweatshop conditions. After witnessing the 1911 **Triangle Shirtwaist Factory fire** that killed 146 workers, she became committed to lobbying for protective labor laws. In 1912, she went to work for the New York Committee on Safety, exposing unsafe conditions and proposing corrective legislation, such as limiting the work week to fifty-four hours.

In 1913, Perkins married economist **Paul Wilson** but retained her maiden name. In 1918, **Governor Alfred E. Smith (1873–1944)** appointed her to a job on the New York State Industrial Commission that paid $8,000 per year, making her the highest-paid state employee in the nation. In 1926, Smith made her industrial commissioner for the state, a position she continued to hold from 1929 to 1932 under Smith's successor, **Franklin D. Roosevelt (1882–1945)**.

When Roosevelt was elected president in 1932, he chose Perkins as his **secretary of labor**, calling her "his most loyal friend," and she was to be one of only two original cabinet appointees to serve from 1933 until his death in 1945. As his **New Deal** policies took shape, Perkins helped draft legislation that was to impact American domestic policy for the next fifty years, including the **Federal Emergency Relief Act**, the Title II public works section of the **National Industrial Recovery Act**, the **Civilian Conservation Corps Act**, the **National Labor Relations Act**, and the **Social Security Act**.

Not only did Perkins help construct New Deal policies, but she tirelessly and skillfully helped to implement them across the country. She also restructured the Department of Labor, ridding the **Immigration and Naturalization Service** of racketeers and establishing the **Division of Labor Standards**. In all instances, her pro-labor stance was evident as she sought to promote the welfare of wage earners.

After Roosevelt's death, Perkins served on the **Civil Service Commission** under **President Harry S. Truman (1884–1972)** from 1945 until 1953, and at age seventy-seven, she became a professor at Cornell University's School of Industrial and Labor Relations, where she taught until she died of a stroke in New York City.

◆ Like **Hypatia** (see no. 10), mathematician **AMALIE EMMY NOETHER** was the daughter of a mathematician and university professor. Known best for her work in **abstract algebra**, she grew up in the university town of Erlangen, Germany, where her father often gathered Emmy and her three younger brothers around him to explain mathematics problems. When the University of Erlangen opened its doors to women, she became one of only two women among 1,000 students, graduating with high honors in 1907 with a doctor of philosophy.

Although German universities admitted women as students, they still did not allow them to become professors. For the next eight years, Noether lived at home, and as her father became increasingly ill, she often taught his classes—without pay—as a substitute teacher. In 1916, **David Hilbert** and **Felix Klein**, who were working on Einstein's **theory of general relativity** at the University of Göttingen, invited her to join their research group. When the university refused to hire a woman, Hilbert made it possible for her to lecture—again, without pay—by announcing her lectures under his own name. Noether, who had a unique ability to work with abstract concepts and visualize complex connections, gained the respect of both the students and faculty. In 1920, she presented a paper on the building up, on an axiomatic basis, of a completely general theory of ideals, a work that was to mark her unique contribution to abstract algebra.

After Adolf Hitler came to power in Germany in 1933, Noether emigrated to the United States and accepted a professorship at Bryn Mawr College near Philadelphia. She also worked at the Institute for Advanced Study in Princeton, New Jersey. When she died unexpectedly of complications following routine surgery at the age of fifty-three, **Albert Einstein (1879–1955)**, who had used her work on the **theory of invariants** in formulating some of his relativity work, eulogized her as "the most significant, creative mathematical genius thus far produced since the higher education of women began."

◆ Probably the most influential and effective woman in twentieth-century American politics, First Lady and social activist **ELEANOR ROOSEVELT**, more than any other woman of her generation, exemplified the personal and political autonomy that were the goals of the women's rights movement. Born in New York City and niece to **President Theodore Roosevelt (1858–1919)**, she attended Allenwood, an exclusive boarding school near London. In 1901, after making her society debut, she joined the **National Consumers League**, evaluating safety conditions in sweatshops, an experience through which she developed a lifelong commitment to political activism.

In 1905, she married her distant cousin, **Franklin D. Roosevelt (1882–1945)** and had five children. Beginning in 1910, when he was elected to the New York Assembly, Eleanor was active in politics. She coordinated the legislative program for the state **League of Women Voters** and worked with the **Women's Trade Union League (WTUL)**

to pass minimum wage laws. When Franklin became paralyzed from polio in 1921, she saved his political career by organizing newly franchised women voters in the state Democratic Party to help elect him governor. By 1928, when she led the national women's campaign for the Democratic Party, she had become a respected political leader in her own right.

During Franklin's first of four successful presidential campaigns in 1932, Eleanor coordinated the women's division of the **Democratic National Committee**. A tireless advocate for the rights of women, minorities, and the disadvantaged, in her first year as First Lady, she traveled over 50,000 miles. She strongly supported the women's division of the **Civil Works Administration**, which provided 100,000 women with jobs, as well as the **National Youth Administration**, the **Social Security Act**, and measures to end racial discrimination in the armed forces. In January 1936, she began a syndicated newspaper column, *My Day*, to share her views. She also prompted her husband to hire qualified women for his administration, such as **Frances Perkins** (see no. 73), leading one newspaper columnist to call Eleanor a "Cabinet Minister without portfolio—the most influential woman of her time."

After her husband's death, **President Harry S. Truman (1884–1972)** appointed Eleanor as a delegate to the **United Nations (UN)**. In 1948, the UN passed the Universal Declaration of Human Rights, a document largely shaped by her, and the entire delegation gave her a standing ovation. Her last official position was to chair the **Commission on the Status of Women** for **President John F. Kennedy (1917–1963)** in 1961. She is the author of *It's Up to Women* (1933) and *This, I Remember* (1949). She died in New York City at the age of seventy-eight.

◆ Born in Hamburg, Germany, and educated at the University of Berlin and the University of Freiburg, child psychoanalyst **KAREN HORNEY** was an instructor at the Berlin Institute for Psychoanalysis for two years before emigrating to the United States in 1932. After serving as an associate director of the Chicago Institute for Psychoanalysis from 1934 to 1941, she taught at the New York Psychoanalytic Institute. In 1941 she cofounded the **American Institute for Psychoanalysis** and served as its dean. The next year she joined the staff of the New York Medical College. Horney founded a **Neo-Freudian school of psychoanalysis**, which stressed that early childhood conflicts and deprivation can lead to neuroses in adulthood. In contrast to Sigmund Freud who stressed the biological basis of neuroses, Horney, a **learning theorist**, believed that the environmental and social aspects of a child's experience played the key roles in personality development.

In her books, *The Neurotic Personality of Our Time* (1937) and *New Ways in Psychoanalysis* (1939), Horney made **basic anxiety** her primary concept. She believed that basic anxiety occurs if a child is treated with coldness and extreme inconsistency by those who raise them. As a result, a child may attempt to cope with these feelings in inappropriate or maladjusted ways. If their anxieties are intense and prolonged, a child's maladaptive methods can become fixed in the form of **neurotic needs**, which Horney defined as being "excessive, insatiable, and unrealistic demands for affection, approval, someone to depend on, power, or personal achievement."

Horney also challenged popular notions about the nature of **masochism**, which claimed that the reason many women were abused by their partners was because they somehow preferred such treatment. She was the first of her profession to state that so-called "natural" feminine masochism was more likely to be the result of a sexist societal system of rewards and punishments that encouraged women to act in extremely passive or overly submissive ways. Her Freudian male colleagues did not appreciate her views and forced her out of the **New York Psychoanalytic Society**. Yet by the 1970s, most mental health professionals came to agree with Horney's viewpoint. She died of abdominal cancer at the age of sixty-seven.

Explorer **LOUISE BOYD** was born in 1887, one of three children to San Francisco mining magnate **John Franklin Boyd**. Left a wealthy heiress at age thirty with no close relatives, she decided to travel. In 1924, she chose a most extraordinary destination: **Spitsbergen**, a small archipelago in the Arctic Sea between Norway and East Greenland, stating she had always been "fond of geography from earliest childhood" with a special interest in "northern latitudes."

On her 1924 trip, the first of seven expeditions to the Arctic, Boyd became the first woman to set foot on **Franz Josef Land**, where she took photographic documentation of every aspect of the landscape. The focus of her 1928 trip became a ten-thousand-mile, three-month search for explorer **Roald Amundsen (1872–1928)**. Although her search proved fruitless, she was decorated by the king of Norway with the **Order of St. Olav**, becoming the first non-Norwegian woman to receive this honor. In 1930, she embarked on a two-month trip to the extreme northern regions of Scandinavia to collect botanical specimens and photograph the native people of the area, the **Sámi people**.

In 1931, Boyd undertook a scientific exploration of the fjords of **East Greenland**, making detailed surveys of typical small areas. Her close study of every fjord and sound in the Franz Josef and King Oscar fjord area revealed errors in previous mappings. Inner reaches of the Ice Fjord that she charted were named **Miss Boyd Land**. The results of her 1933 expedition were published as *The Fjord Region of East Greenland*. On her 1937 outing, Boyd mapped another new region, which was named **Louise Boyd Bank**. Her greatest triumph came during her 1938 expedition when she landed her steamship *Veslekari* farther up the East Greenland shore than any other American ever had.

Calling her "the only woman to achieve an outstanding position in Arctic exploration," the **American Geographical Society** awarded her the **Cullum Medal** in 1938 and elected her to the **Council of Fellows**, the first woman in its 108-year history. Details of her explorations can be found in E. F. Olds' book *Women of the Four Winds* (1985).

During **World War II**, the U.S. government considered Boyd's data to be of such strategic military importance that she had to postpone publication of her book, *The Coast of Northeast Greenland*, until 1948. She also served as a consultant to military intelligence in Washington in 1942. When she died at the age of eighty-four, her ashes were scattered over the Arctic as per her wishes.

LUCILA GODEY ALCAYA (GABRIELA MISTRAL)
1889–1957

◆ Poet and diplomat **LUCILA GODEY ALCAYA** (pen name: **Gabriela Mistral**) was born in the Elqui Valley village of Vicuna in northern Chile and brought up by her mother, a schoolteacher. From this humble beginning, she became one of the most celebrated and influential South American writers of the twentieth century and a symbol of the nationalist aspirations of her country.

After studying education, child welfare, and labor issues, Mistral taught in rural secondary schools, and in 1912, she became the director of the Liceo de Los Andes in Punta Arenas in southern Chile. Upon publication of her first sonnets "Sonetos de la muerte" in 1914, she became known for her poetry, which critics said displayed a "visionary, prophetic sense of the destiny of Latin America." In 1922, her collection *Desolacion* appeared, and she was also sent by the government to study educational and library systems in Mexico for two years, where she collaborated on a national educational reform program. Upon her return home in 1924, she was honored for her work. Later that year, *Ternura* was published.

In 1925, Mistral began a second career as a diplomat when she was named as the Chilean delegate to the **United Nations**, where she became head of the **Cultural Committee** and the **Committee of the Institute of International Intellectual Cooperation** in Paris between 1926 and 1939. After serving as the **Chilean Consul** in Madrid in 1934, she was made a "life consul" and later worked in posts in Lisbon, Portugal; Nice, France; Rio de Janeiro, Brazil; and Los Angeles, California, United States. In 1944, she was diagnosed with diabetes and moved to the United States for her health, where she served as a cultural attaché. Following a thirteen-year hiatus in her writing, Mistral published two books of poems, *Tala* (1938) and *Lagar* (1954). She also wrote several novels about Chilean life. In her many books, theses, and poems, Mistral seemed devoted to an intellectual and spiritual quest. As M. A. de Vázquez relates in the book *Gabriela Mistral: The Poet and Her Work* (1964), Mistral was haunted by grief from the suicide of her first love in 1909 and that of her nephew, whom she had adopted. Thus, her work, "while reflecting deeply private feelings, seemed to speak with a voice that all humanity could understand." Although she closely identified with her country, so much so that she once stated, "I am and will remain, a daughter of my land," she nonetheless acknowledged her diverse influences, including Spanish, Russian, and Indian writers along with Christian and Buddhist philosophers.

In 1945, Gabriela Mistral became the first South American writer to receive the **Nobel Prize in Literature**.

Born in Torquay, England, celebrated mystery author and playwright **AGATHA CHRISTIE** was a prolific writer who, over a span of more than fifty years, penned 68 novels, 17 plays, and more than 100 short stories that have been published in 103 languages throughout the world. She first became interested in mystery stories as a young girl when her sister Madge introduced her to the adventures of **Sir Arthur Conan Doyle's (1859–1930)** cerebral sleuth Sherlock Holmes. Christie began writing after she left school, completing her first short story, "The House of Beauty," when she was 18. In 1913, she met Archie Christie, an army officer, at a dance. The two fell in love and married the following year. From 1914 to 1918, while her husband was deployed during World War I, Christie volunteered for the war effort. She worked at a Red Cross hospital first as a nurse, and after eventually qualifying as an apothecaries' assistant, worked as a dispenser.

In 1920, when she was twenty-nine, Christie publisher her first detective novel, *The Mysterious Affair at Styles*. Christie's stories are well known for their lively cast of colorful characters and intricate plots twists. She also invented two very memorable detectives. The fictional **Hercule Poirot**, an eccentric Belgian detective who solves puzzles presented to him by using his "little gray cells" to make deductions, first appeared in *The Mysterious Affair at Styles*. When Christie killed off Poirot in *Curtain* (1975), his death made the front page of the *New York Times*. **Miss Jane Marple**, Christie's other well-known sleuth, was an elderly spinster who ferreted out murderers in her small village of St. Mary's Mead. She made her debut in 1930 in *Murder at the Vicarage* and continued her pursuit of elusive murderers until her final appearance in *Sleeping Murder* (1976), which was published after Christie's death.

On a trip to the Middle East in 1930, Christie met her second husband, archaeologist **Sir Max Mallowan (1904–1978)**. She subsequently accompanied him on his yearly digs in Iraq and Syria. From these travels sprang her novels *Murder in Mesopotamia* (1935), *Death on the Nile* (1937), and *Appointment with Death* (1938). *Agatha Christie: An Autobiography*, appeared in 1977.

Christie's play, *The Mousetrap*, which opened at the Ambassador Theater in London in 1952, has been continuously performed ever since, making it the world's longest-running theatrical production. Another play, *Witness for the Prosecution* (1953), received the **New York Drama Critics' Circle Award** in 1954. In 1971, **Queen Elizabeth II (b. 1926)** appointed her a Dame of the British Empire.

◆ The most influential and innovative figure in modern dance for over fifty years, **MARTHA GRAHAM** was born in Pittsburgh, Pennsylvania, but grew up in California. At age twenty, she studied ethnic and primitive dance at Denishawn in Hollywood, where director **Ted Shawn**, recognizing her remarkable talent, created the ballet *Xochitl* on an Aztec theme for her. From 1923 to 1925, she danced in the Greenwich Village Follies, and in 1926, she taught at the Eastman School of Music, where she began to explore how dance could "give substance to the things she felt."

Graham launched her career as an independent dancer and choreographer in a solo debut at the **48th Street Theatre** in New York that shocked and amazed the audience. Unlike traditional ballet, Graham's movements were angular, taut, and low to the ground, and they consisted of intense thrusts of movement outward from the center of her body to express emotions. She founded the **Dance Repertory Theatre** and quickly established a reputation for providing the most strenuous training in the field. Her unique teaching method emphasized contracting and releasing different parts of the body and using the breath in relation to movement.

Graham's works centered on the universal experiences of humankind and on the themes of love, death, and the cyclical nature of life. From 1928 to 1938—which she called "the period of long woolens"—she choreographed works on protest themes, such as her works *Revolt, Immigrant, Lamentation,* and *Primitive Mysteries*. In 1932, she became the first dancer to receive a Guggenheim Fellowship. She created a number of dances based on famous women like Joan of Arc and Mary, Queen of Scots and explored in depth the psyches of Emily Dickinson (*Letter to the World,* 1940) and the Brontë sisters (*Deaths and Entrances,* 1943). She also produced Greek drama and myth inspired pieces, including *Cave of the Heart* (1946) about Medea; *Night Journey* about Oedipus' mother, Jocasta; and the first full-length modern dance work ever written, *Clytemnestra* (1958). After 1938, she used music only expressly composed for her dances by such famous composers as **Aaron Copland (1900–1990)** (*Appalachian Spring,* 1944), **Gian Carlo Menotti (1911–2007)**, and **Samuel Barber (1910–1981)**.

Graham, who choreographed 180 works and enjoyed the longest active career of any modern dancer, retired from the stage in 1969 to become a full-time teacher, lecturer, and director of the **Martha Graham Center for Contemporary Dance** in New York. She received numerous honors, including the **Presidential Medal of Freedom** in 1976. She died in New York City at the age of ninety-seven.

Born in Vienna, Austria, the daughter of the founder of psychoanalysis, **Sigmund Freud (1856–1939), ANNA FREUD** is most well known for her pioneering work in the field of child psychoanalysis. After working as a children's teacher, she collaborated with her father on the development of **psychoanalytic theory**. In her method, which came to be known as the **Vienna School**, the therapist interprets the meaning of play to the child and greater emphasis is placed on the therapist's educational role with the family.

In 1938, Anna and her father fled to England to avoid Nazi persecution where, after Sigmund's death, Anna continued to utilize and expand upon his theories. In 1945, she helped to launch the annual periodical *Psychoanalytic Study of the Child*, and in 1947, she opened the **Hampstead Child Therapy Course and Clinic** in London, later serving as its director in 1952. The term "defense" was first used by Sigmund Freud in 1894 to describe the ego's struggle with pain. But it was only with Anna Freud's *The Ego and Mechanisms of Defense* (1946) that **defense mechanisms** achieved the importance they deserved in both theory and therapy. This groundbreaking book marks the beginning of **ego psychology**. Psychoanalysts turned from concentrating solely on interpreting the unconscious to the patient to placing an equal emphasis upon discovering and interpreting the various defense mechanisms that a patient uses to avoid feeling pain or anxiety. According to Anna Freud, defense mechanisms include denial, repression, introjection, projection, displacement, reaction formation, isolation, undoing, regression, fixation, and intellectualization.

Freud stressed that all defense mechanisms also had a positive side and are a necessary part of personality development.

She believed they became harmful to a person's psychological well-being only when overused, at which point they can distort a person's view of reality and impede further healthy psychological growth.

Freud also studied the nature of **separation anxiety** in infants (*Infants Without Families*, 1944) and feeding disorders (1946), the latter of which she classified into "organic," "nonorganic disturbances of the instinctive process itself," and "neurotic feeding disturbances." Many aspects of her work also extended to family law, where she emphasized the importance of the psychological bond between a parent and child.

Upon her first return to Vienna in 1971, she was given a standing ovation at the 27th International Psychoanalytical Congress. The following year, Vienna University became one of many institutions to award her an honorary doctorate.

◆ Born in Philadelphia, Pennsylvania, the daughter of a coal and ice merchant, contralto **MARIAN ANDERSON** was destined to become a legend not only for her magnificent, three-octave voice, but also as the first African American opera singer to break through major racial barriers.

Anderson began singing in her church choir at age six, and at age twenty-two, she entered a vocal contest, which she won among 300 other singers, giving her the opportunity to perform with the **New York Philharmonic Orchestra**. She embarked on a European concert tour culminating at the 1935 Salzburg Festival in Austria, where conductor **Arturo Toscanini (1867–1957)** welcomed her by exclaiming that her voice was "such as one hears once in a hundred years."

Although she returned to America as an internationally renowned celebrity, Anderson was still limited to performing in segregated halls. In 1939, the **Daughters of the American Revolution (DAR)** would not allow her to present a recital in Philadelphia's Constitution Hall, claiming that the date she requested had already been taken. When **First Lady Eleanor Roosevelt** (see no. 75) learned of this, she resigned from the organization and arranged for Anderson to give an open-air concert at the **Lincoln Memorial** in Washington, DC, on Easter Sunday. Her performance, which included spirituals, Schubert's *Ave Maria* and the national anthem, drew more than 75,000 people, the largest public tribute since **Charles Lindbergh (1902–1974)** returned home a decade earlier.

Although she felt uncomfortable about the performance, as she wrote in her 1956 autobiography *My Lord, What a Morning*, she prevailed, saying: "I could see that my significance as an individual was small in this affair. I had become, whether I liked it

or not, a symbol, representing my people. I had to appear."

President Franklin D. Roosevelt (1882–1945) later invited Anderson to sing for King George VI at the White House, making her the first Black artist to sing there. In January 1955, she made her debut with the **Metropolitan Opera**, opening the way for an entire generation of Black artists, including **Leontyne Price, Jessye Norman**, and **Kathleen Battle**.

In 1958, **President Dwight D. Eisenhower (1890–1969)** appointed Anderson to the Human Rights Committee of the United Nations, and in 1961, she sang at **John F. Kennedy's (1917–1963)** inauguration. In 1963, she received the **Presidential Medal of Freedom**. In April 1993, one month after suffering a stroke, she died in her home in Danbury, Connecticut, at the age of ninety-one.

Daring American aviator **AMELIA EARHART** became a national heroine in 1928 when she became the first woman to cross the Atlantic Ocean alone by air. She later chronicled her experience in *20 Hours, 40 Minutes* (1928). She withdrew from Columbia University to earn money for flying lessons and worked as the aviation editor at *Cosmopolitan* magazine. She founded **The Ninety-Nines**, an international organization of women pilots. Though her flying career was brief, her numerous accomplishments—including being the first woman to receive the **Distinguished Flying Cross**—still stand as an inspiration.

Earhart was only a passenger on that first historic flight, having accepted an invitation from pilots **Wilmer Stultz** and **Lewis Gordon** to accompany them on their transatlantic journey, but in 1932, she became the first woman to fly solo over the Atlantic. Her time of thirteen hours and thirty minutes set a record, for which she was awarded honors by both the American and French governments. In 1935, she became the first woman to fly over the Pacific Ocean when she crossed from Hawaii to California. Later that year, she set a speed record, flying nonstop from Mexico City to New York City in fourteen hours and nineteen minutes.

On May 21, 1937, accompanied by navigator **Fred Noonan**, her husband **George Putnam (1887–1950)** and mechanic **Bo McNeeley**, Earhart took off from Oakland, California, in a *Lockheed Electra Model 10E*. Her intention was to become the first woman to circumnavigate the globe via the equator. When the plane refueled in Miami, Putnam and McNeeley left the flight, and Earhart and Noonan continued to fly east.

In 1987, **Carol Osborne**, together with Earhart's sister **Grace Muriel Earhart Morrissey**, wrote *Amelia, My Courageous Sister*. According to Osborne's research, which included numerous personal interviews, Earhart took off from Lae, Papua New Guinea, on July 1, 1937, heading toward Howland Island. Radio experts aboard the *Itasca*, a U.S. Coast Guard ship awaiting her arrival, picked up this transmission: "We are circling but cannot hear you." Due to the strength of the signal, *Itasca* personnel believed she was close to Howland. An hour later at 8:46 a.m. Howland time, after Earhart had been in the air twenty hours and sixteen minutes, she sent her last transmission: "We are on the line position 157–337... are running north and south."

When Earhart's plane disappeared, the Navy conducted an exhaustive search of the area until July 18, but to this day, no wreckage has ever been found. What happened? Many theories have been advanced over the years, but Earhart family members and Osborne maintain that Amelia's plane ran out of fuel and she and Noonan died at sea. However, despite Osborne's well-researched book, Earhart's disappearance remains one of the most intriguing mysteries of the twentieth century.

A politician of incomparable stature and the first woman prime minister of Israel, **GOLDA MABOVITCH** was born in Kyiv, Ukraine, then emigrated to Milwaukee, Wisconsin, in 1905. She attended the Teachers Training College in Milwaukee in 1917 and, in the same year, married **Morris Myerson** (later modifying this name to the Hebrew **Meir**). Active in the **Labor Zionist Party**, she and her husband emigrated to Palestine (later Israel) in 1921, where they joined the **Kibbutz Merhavia**. In 1923, they settled in Tel Aviv, and she worked as a treasurer in the Office of Public Works of the **Histradrut**, a labor federation.

In 1928, Meir became secretary of the **Women's Labor Council** in Palestine and was elected as a delegate to congresses of the **World Zionist Organization**. After serving on the **Jewish National Council** and on the board of directors of several Histradrut aid programs, in 1940, she was appointed head of the Histradrut's political department. She continued in this role until Israel's independence was declared on May 14, 1948, when, as a member of the **Provisional Council of State**, she became one of the signers of Israel's **Declaration of Independence**. She then served as the first Israeli minister to the USSR for six months.

In January 1949, Meir was elected to the first Israeli Knesset, or Israeli Parliament, as a Mapai Party representative, and **Prime Minister Ben Gurion** appointed her **minister of labor and national insurance**, making her the only woman in his administration. While in this office, she successfully resolved the sensitive issues of housing and employment for the mass of immigrants pouring into the newly formed Jewish state. In 1956, she became **minister of foreign affairs**, a position she held for ten years. Meir also chaired the Israeli delegation to the **United Nations** from 1953 to 1966. For the next two years, she served as secretary-general of the Mapai Party, and during this time she was able to reunite the three main party elements: Mapai, Achdut Ha'Avodah, and Rafi. Eight months after the merger, she retired from political office.

Upon the death of **Prime Minister Levi Eshkol** in March 1969, Meir was asked to act as an interim prime minister and went on to be elected to the office in October of that year. During the next six years, she built a solid international reputation as a tough-minded but empathetic leader. She resigned in 1974 after controversy arose over Israel's lack of preparedness for the Yom Kippur War of October 1973. Her autobiography, *My Life*, was published in 1975. She died in Jerusalem at the age of eighty.

Anthropologist **MARGARET MEAD's** father was a professor of economics at the University of Pennsylvania, and her mother was a sociologist who had studied Italian immigrants. At Barnard College, she was influenced by anthropologists who believed that patterns of behavior were culturally transmitted (**"nurture"**) rather than genetically inherited (**"nature"**).

In the summer of 1925, Mead went to **Ta'u Island** in **American Samoa** to conduct a field study. For nine months she interviewed natives about their family life and sexual behavior. Her book, *Coming of Age in Samoa* (1928), strongly supported "nurture" as being the major determinant of human behavior. Until Mead's study, the role of women in society, child-rearing practices, and questions about how values and traditions were handed down from one generation to the next had been largely ignored by anthropologists. Her book not only secured her reputation as a nationally prominent intellectual, but its frank advocacy of sexual freedom, though written in a scientific context, made it a bestseller.

Mead conducted several other field studies, including one of the **Manus** people of the **Admiralty Islands** near **Papua New Guinea** (*Growing Up in New Guinea*, 1930), where, to measure the mental functioning of children, she pioneered the use of psychological tests such as drawings. She is considered the founder of the **culture and personality school**, which focuses on the ways that cultures shape personality, and she advanced the documentary use of photography and later video.

In 1926, Mead became the assistant curator of ethnology at the **American Museum of Natural History** in New York, holding various posts there until becoming curator emeritus in 1970. From 1948 to 1950, she was director of research in contemporary cultures at Columbia University and an adjunct professor after 1954. In 1969, she became a full professor and head of the social science department at Fordham University. In the 1960s and 1970s, she was a frequent interview guest on radio and television and gave numerous lectures. Using a jargon-free, novelistic style of writing, Mead produced over two dozen works, including *Sex and Temperament in Three Primitive Societies* (1935), *Male and Female* (1949), *Culture and Commitment: A Study of the Generation Gap* (1970), along with her autobiography *Blackberry Winter* (1972).

On November 15, 1978, the day the *World Almanac* named her one of the world's twenty-five most influential women, Margaret Mead died of pancreatic cancer in New York City at the age of seventy-seven.

Considered the leading American woman photojournalist of the twentieth century, **MARGARET BOURKE-WHITE** was born in New York City, the second child of an engineer-designer. She entered Rutgers University at seventeen to study engineering and biology and graduated from Cornell University in 1927, where she supported herself by selling idyllic pictures of campus life.

Like many photographers of the 1920s and 1930s, Bourke-White's work celebrated machines and the technological age. In 1927, she moved to Cleveland, where she specialized in architectural and industrial subjects, which she described as "sincere and unadorned in their beauty." In 1929, she joined the staff of the new magazine *Fortune*, beginning a lifelong association with the publications of **Henry R. Luce (1898–1967)**, which included *Time* and *Life* magazines. The direction of her career changed dramatically after she produced a social documentary piece for *Fortune* on the Midwest's drought-stricken **Dust Bowl** titled "The Drought" in October 1934. Moved by what she saw, she began to photograph the human experience.

In 1935, Bourke-White joined the staff of Luce's new showcase for photojournalism, which was *Life* magazine. Sent to cover a Montana dam project, she produced a human-interest piece on nearby frontier towns on her own initiative. Luce subsequently used this material for the cover picture and lead article in the first issue of the magazine on November 23, 1936.

That same year Bourke-White collaborated with writer **Erskine Caldwell (1903–1987)** on a haunting portrait of Southern sharecroppers. Considered a landmark documentary, *You Have Seen Their Faces* (1937) is her most historically significant work. During their brief marriage between 1939 and 1942, the couple also produced *North of the Danube* (1939) on Czechoslovakia before the war and *Say, Is This the U.S.A.* (1941).

During **World War II**, Bourke-White became the first female war correspondent accredited by the military.. Often ending up on the front lines, she accompanied **General George Patton (1885–1945)** and the Third Army to record the last days of the **Third Reich**. Entering the death camps, she produced *The Living Dead of Buchenwald*, a classic in the history of photography. Bourke-White's postwar assignments were covering India and the Korean War, where she focused on the human-interest aspects rather than guerrilla fighting. By the mid-1950s, she had reached the peak of her profession. After she contracted Parkinson's Disease, she documented her rehabilitation as an encouragement to others. She died in Stamford, Connecticut. Her autobiography, *Portrait of Myself*, was published in 1963.

When she was a young girl growing up in Springdale, Pennsylvania, **RACHEL CARSON** was greatly influenced by her mother, **Maria Carson**, a schoolteacher who shared her deep love of nature with her. Later, as a marine biologist committed to preserving the beauty of the earth, she wrote *Silent Spring* (1962), a landmark book which focused the attention of the world on environmental dangers and helped launch the environmental protection movement.

After graduating magna cum laude, or with great honors, from Pennsylvania College for Women, Carson received a master of arts degree from Johns Hopkins University in 1932. She worked summers at the **Marine Biological Laboratory** in Massachusetts, and in 1935, became one of the first two women staff biologists at the **U.S. Bureau of Fisheries**. Her 1937 article for *The Atlantic Monthly* titled "Undersea" later became her first book, *Under the Sea-Wind* (1941).

During **World War II**, Carson worked for the **U.S. Fish and Wildlife Service**, and by 1949, she was chief editor of their publishing program. Her second book, *The Sea Around Us* (1951), first serialized in the *New Yorker* magazine, became an immediate bestseller, was awarded the **National Book Award**, and was eventually translated into 32 languages.

After years of struggling to financially support her mother and two orphaned nieces, Carson received a Guggenheim Foundation fellowship in 1951, which allowed her to take a leave of absence for a year from her job. Her next book, *The Edge of the Sea* (1955), solidified her reputation as an articulate interpreter of natural science. In 1957, after her niece died, Carson adopted her five-year-old son, **Roger Christie,** who served as an inspiration for a 1956 magazine article, "Help Your Child to Wonder."

The article was published after her death as an illustrated children's book, *The Sense of Wonder*.

The precipitating event to Carson's most famous work, *Silent Spring*, was a request for help from a friend who had witnessed the wholesale destruction of wildlife in her bird sanctuary after it had been sprayed with pesticides. Using data gathered from scientists throughout America and Europe, Carson wrote a searing indictment of the indiscriminate use of toxic chemicals and the irresponsibility of industrialized societies toward the earth and its resources. As a direct result of her expose, **President John F. Kennedy (1917–1963)** formed a special panel to study the effects of pesticides on the environment.

Rachel Carson died of bone cancer in 1964 in Silver Spring, Maryland. By 1972, the United States government banned all domestic use of DDT.

AGNES GONXHA BEJAXHIA was born to Albanian parents in the town of Skopje, Macedonia. At the age of eighteen, she entered the Roman Catholic Order of the **Sisters of Loreto** in Ireland. After she received training in Dublin, Ireland, and Darjeeling, India, she took her vows to become a nun.

In 1929, as **Sister Teresa**, she became part of a group of Loreto nuns in Calcutta (now Kolkata) and taught high school there for nearly twenty years. While working as a teacher, she was deeply moved by the incredible suffering of the sick and dying she encountered daily on the crowded city streets. On September 10, 1946, while riding a train in Darjeeling, she received what she believed to be a clear call from God to leave the Sisters of Loreto and to devote her life to working for the impoverished of the city while living among them.

Granted permission by the Pope to leave her post at the convent, Mother Teresa began her lifelong ministry among the poor in 1948. Two years later, she and her workers were approved by the archdiocese of Calcutta as the new order of the **Missionaries of Charity**. The order was later recognized as a pontifical congregation under the direct jurisdiction of Rome. Women joining this religious community took four vows upon acceptance. In addition to the traditional clerical vows of poverty, chastity, and obedience, Missionaries of Charity took a fourth vow pledging service to the poor.

The basic belief underlying Mother Teresa's work was that the poor symbolized Christ and that, by serving them, she and her sisters were serving Christ. The sisters saw their primary mission as a religious one, although they carried out their work in various ways as nurses and social workers.

In 1952, Mother Teresa opened the **Nirmal Hriday ("Place for the Pure of Heart")** in Calcutta. By the end of her life, she had extended her work to five continents, operating 517 missions in over 100 countries. Her book about her life, *Gift from God*, was published in 1975. In recognition of her achievements, she was awarded the **1975 Nobel Peace Prize**, and in 1985, she received the **Presidential Medal of Freedom** from the United States. After several years of poor health, Mother Teresa died in 1997 at the age of eighty-seven. She was beatified in 2003 and canonized as a saint by Pope Francis in 2015.

◆ Named "the greatest woman athlete of the first half of the twentieth century" in a 1950 Associated Press poll, women's sports pioneer **MILDRED ELLA DIDRIKSON** was born in Port Arthur, Texas, the fourth of seven children of Norwegian immigrants. Her father was a carpenter, and her mother was a practical nurse and amateur athlete.

Didrikson's performance on the Beaumont High School basketball team caught the attention of **Melvin McCombs**, who recruited her for his company-sponsored Amateur Athletic Union (AAU) team. After the team won the national championship, Didrikson took up track. She competed in eight events in the 1932 **National AAU Track & Field Championships**, winning five, tying one, and accumulating enough points to win the team championship by herself. At the **1932 Olympic Games** in Los Angeles, limited to three events, she became an **Olympic gold medalist** and set records in the javelin (143 feet, 4 inches) and the 80-meter hurdles (11.7 seconds), and won a silver medal for high jump.

Didrikson next took up golf and won the **Texas Women's Championship** in 1934. Less than a month later, she was ruled ineligible for amateur competition because she had accepted money in other sports. In 1938, Didrikson married wrestler **George Zaharias** and regained her amateur status. She then won an unprecedented seventeen consecutive golf tournaments, including the **U.S. Women's Amateur Championship**, the **World Championship**, and the **U.S. Women's Open**. In 1947, she became the first American to win the **British Ladies Amateur**.

Following this success, Didrikson turned professional. With her husband's advice and financial support, she began to lay the groundwork for professional women's competition in golf. In 1948, she and five other women golfers created the **Ladies Professional Golf Association (LPGA)**, recruiting a sporting goods company as a sponsor for the initial set of tournaments. Didrikson's tenacity showed when she was stricken with cancer. In 1955, just fifteen months after major surgery, she won her third U.S. Open title.

A gifted athlete, Didrikson's talent and widespread popularity helped to dispel existing myths about the competitive ability of women athletes, thus opening the door for more women to compete in a wider variety of professional sports. Didrikson's autobiography, *This Life I've Led*, was published in 1955. The following year, her cancer recurred, and she died at the age of forty-two.

◆ Known as "the first lady of civil rights," **ROSA PARKS'** refusal to give up her bus seat to a white man sparked the **Montgomery bus boycott** in 1955, which was the catalyst for the **American civil rights movement** of the 1960s.

Born in Tuskegee, Alabama, she married barber **Raymond Parks** in 1932. In 1943, she was one of the first women to join the Montgomery chapter of the **National Association for the Advancement of Colored People (NAACP)**, where she served as a youth advisor and secretary from 1943 to 1956 as well as office manager for NAACP State President **Edgar Nixon**.

In 1955, Montgomery public buses were segregated by law. On Thursday, December 1, 1955, Parks, who was on her way home from her tailoring job, was sitting in the first row of the designated Black section of a bus. When a white man boarded, the bus driver asked four Black passengers to move and give the white man a seat. Three did, but Rosa Parks refused. The driver called the police, who arrested and jailed her.

Because seventy-five percent of the bus ridership was Black, African American community leaders decided that a boycott would make a powerful economic impact, and Parks agreed to allow her December 5 trial to become the focus of the fight against segregation. On December 2, 52,000 fliers were distributed, calling for a one-day bus boycott on the day of her trial. The boycott was so successful that it was continued indefinitely. After Parks was found guilty and fined $10, she refused to pay and appealed her conviction.

Parks and her husband soon lost their jobs, and she then helped organize carpools to maintain the boycott. Though Black people were harassed and threatened, the boycott continued. In 1956, after the **Montgomery Improvement Association** filed suit, the U.S. District Court declared segregated seating on public buses unconstitutional, a decision upheld by the U.S. Supreme Court. After 381 days, the bus boycott ended in success. In 1957, Parks moved to Detroit, Michigan, where she continued her civil rights work with the **Southern Christian Leadership Conference (SCLC)**, which has annually sponsored the **Rosa Parks Freedom Award** since 1963. Between 1965 and 1988, she worked as a staff assistant to U.S. Representative **John Conyers**. The recipient of many honorary degrees and awards, Parks was the first woman to receive the **Martin Luther King Jr. Nonviolent Peace Prize** in 1980, and the city of Detroit named a boulevard and arts center after her. In 1987, she established the **Rosa and Raymond Parks Institute for Self Development** to work with teens. In 1990, 3,000 government and community leaders gathered at the Kennedy Center in Washington, DC, to celebrate her seventy-fifth birthday. She died in 2005 at the age of ninety-two.

One of the most tenacious and influential political leaders of her time, India's first woman prime minister, **INDIRA PRIYADARSHINI NEHRU**, was born in Allahabad, the only child of **Jawaharlal Nehru (1889–1964)**, India's first prime minister. After attending school in Switzerland and England, she married childhood friend and journalist **Feroze Gandhi (d. 1960)**. Upon returning to India in 1942, they were imprisoned for thirteen months for their support of the nationalist movement. They had two sons, Rajiv and Sanjay.

Growing up, Gandhi had known most of the leaders of the nationalist struggle for freedom, including **Mohandas "Mahatma" Gandhi (1869–1948)** (no relation). After Britain granted independence to India in 1947, she served as her father's hostess and confidant for eighteen years until his death in 1964. Throughout this time, she was active in numerous social and political organizations, serving as chairperson of the **Central Social Welfare Board** from 1953 to 1957 and president of the **Indian Youth Congress** from 1956 to 1960. She was also a member of the **Congress Working Committee** and the **Central Election Committee**. When her father died, she was elected to his seat in Parliament. In 1964, **Prime Minister Lal Shastri** appointed her **minister of information and broadcasting**. When he died two years later, she was elected leader of the Congress Party and became India's third prime minister. After party members opposed to her policies split the party, Gandhi called a general election in 1971, tirelessly touring the country to gain public support, and was elected by a large margin.

At the peak of her power, Gandhi experienced a series of setbacks. Growing economic difficulties sparked demonstrations in 1974, and she declared emergency rule, imprisoning political adversaries and severely censoring the press—measures seen by some as violating the constitution. In the March 1977 elections, she was turned out of office. In October 1977, she was jailed briefly on charges of official corruption, and fourteen months later, she was expelled from Parliament. Following this, she reorganized her party and was re-elected prime minister in a landslide victory in the election of January 1980.

On the world front, Gandhi became a forceful spokesperson for developing nations, but she continued to face sectarian opposition at home. In 1983 and 1984, she sent government troops to quell disturbances in the Punjab, where they sacked a **Sikh** temple. In retaliation, Gandhi was assassinated by two of her Sikh bodyguards at her residence in New Delhi in June of 1984. Her son Rajiv was immediately sworn in as prime minister.

◆ Known to many as the mother of the modern women's movement, **BETTY GOLDSTEIN** was born in Peoria, Illinois. Her mother was a journalist who abandoned her career when she married—a fact that played a key role in the development of Friedan's feminist beliefs. She studied at Smith College and the University of California at Berkeley. In 1947, she married **Carl Friedan**, a theatrical producer, and became a full-time homemaker for their three children. Feeling unfulfilled while living the supposedly ideal life of a suburban New York housewife, Friedan wrote her now classic 1963 book, *The Feminine Mystique*, which debunked the 1950s myth of the "happy homemaker." It sold 65,000 hardback and 700,000 paperback copies in the first year. When *Mystique* appeared, the average age for women to marry in the United States was 19.8 years old and ninety-three percent were married by the age of 30. Friedan identified "the problem that has no name" as resulting from the "feminine mystique"—the stereotype perpetuated by society, and reinforced in the press, that the only rewarding role for a woman was to sacrifice her individual identity and submerge herself in the role of a wife and mother. The result, Friedan asserted, was that in middle age, many women felt empty. She recommended that women seek professional careers where they could use their intellect and talents.

Friedan was one of many twentieth-century women to articulate the issue of women's constricted role in society. In 1941, **Pearl S. Buck (1892–1973)**—winner of the Nobel Prize in Literature for *The Good Earth* (1938)—wrote *Of Men and Women*. Although this book went largely unnoticed because it was published in November 1941 when nearly all news and media in the United States revolved around World War II, it exposed the myth that women had freedom and opportunity and called for equal access in education and work. Another book that traced the nature of women's oppression through the ages was the massive two-volume study *The Second Sex* (1949) by French philosopher and author **Simone de Beauvoir (1908–1986)**, which appeared at a time when most women were content with postwar affluence. Friedan's book became a catalyst for the women's liberation movement because it appeared in the 1960s, a decade of massive social change when women were ready to take action. In 1966, Friedan founded the **National Organization for Women (NOW)** to ensure the adoption and enforcement of women's rights legislation, serving as president until 1970. She also helped organize the **National Women's Political Caucus** in 1971, led the 1970 nationwide **Women's Strike for Equality**, convened the **International Feminist Planning Congress** in 1973, and helped found New York's **First Women's Bank** (now New York Bank for Business) the same year. Her other works include *The Second Stage* (1981) and *Fountain of Age* (1993). She died in 2006 on her eighty-sixth birthday.

SHIRLEY ST. HILL CHISHOLM, an outspoken and independent legislator, became the first African American woman to be elected to the **U.S. Congress** in 1968. Four years later, she became the first Black person to seek a major party nomination for president.

Born in the Bedford-Stuyvesant neighborhood of Brooklyn, New York, Chisholm and her sisters went to live with their maternal grandmother in Barbados for seven years while her impoverished parents saved money for their children's futures as they strongly believed in the importance of education. Chisholm studied at Brooklyn College to become a teacher, graduating *cum laude*, and received a **master of arts degree** in elementary education at Columbia University, where she met and then married **Conrad Chisholm**.

In 1953, having worked as a teacher in a childcare center and as director of a nursery school, Chisholm joined the **New York City Bureau of Child Welfare**. She also became active with the **Seventeenth Assembly District Democratic Club**, where she helped form the **Unity Democratic Club** to work for reforms in the district's political machine. In 1964, she ran for the New York State Assembly and won by a comfortable margin of 18,151 to 1893 and 913 votes in a three-way contest.

After Congressional district lines were redrawn in 1968, Chisholm ran for the seat from the new, primarily Black, twelfth district. She won by 1,000 votes and went on to be re-elected six more times before she retired in 1982. While in the **U.S. House of Representatives**, she earned a reputation as a maverick, often crossing party lines when voting. At the 1972 Democratic Convention, she received 151 delegate votes in her bid against George McGovern for the party nomination.

In 1982, Chisholm became a professor at Mount Holyoke College, and in 1985, she was a visiting scholar at Spelman College. In 1984, she founded the **National Political Congress of Black Women (NPCBW)**, and in 1988, the group sent a delegation of 100 women to the Democratic Convention to present demands for promoting civil rights and social programs. Instead of being remembered for her "firsts," Chisholm stated that she would rather be remembered "as a catalyst for change, a woman who had the determination... [and] perseverance to fight on behalf of the female population and the Black population, because I'm a product of both." In 1993, **President Bill Clinton (b. 1946)** appointed her U.S. ambassador to Jamaica. She has served as a major influence for many women of color in politics, including Vice President Kamala Harris, who wore purple to her 2021 inauguration as a nod to Chisholm.

Britain's first woman prime minister, **MARGARET ROBERTS THATCHER**, was born in Grantham, Lincolnshire, England, the daughter of a prominent grocer and Methodist lay preacher who twice served as town mayor. In 1947, she graduated from Somerville College at the University of Oxford with a degree in chemistry, and for the next four years, she worked as a research chemist for a Colchester plastics firm and for J. Lyons & Company.

When she was twenty-two, she pursued her first public office as a candidate in Dartford. In 1951, she married **Sir Denis Thatcher**, who managed his family's paint business, and left her job to pursue a degree in law, taking the bar exam in 1953 after an unusually short time. That same year she gave birth to twins, a son and a daughter. Afterward, she worked as a tax lawyer until she won a seat in Parliament for Finchley, London in 1959.

From 1961 to 1964, she served as **joint parliamentary secretary** for the **Ministry of Pensions and National Insurance** and became **secretary of state for education and science** when her party won the election. In 1974, she was elected leader of the **Conservative Party**, and in 1979 she led her party to victory, becoming the first woman prime minister in Britain's history. Thatcher once expressed her philosophy of leadership thusly: "There can be no liberty unless there is economic liberty... Extinguish free enterprise and you extinguish liberty." Her fiscal policies included attacking inflation by reducing the money supply, reducing public spending, and raising interest rates. In 1982, her hardline stance at home, as well as abroad—as evidenced by her outspoken stand against the USSR's invasion of Afghanistan—earned her the nickname of **The Iron Lady**. The quick military intervention

that she ordered following Argentina's invasion of the **Falkland Islands** in 1982 also won her high praise.

Thatcher's second term of office in 1983 was marked by confrontations with major unions. Her policies led to a reduction in the inflation rate from 24 percent in 1979 to 3.5 percent, and her encouragement of privatization programs led to the creation of several major public companies, such as British Gas and British Airways.

In 1987, Thatcher became the first British prime minister in the twentieth century to win three consecutive terms, and she came to be regarded as an elder stateswoman, having built close ties with other major world leaders. In 1990, after losing support within her own party, she resigned as prime minister, although she continued to serve in Parliament until 1992. Her autobiography, *The Downing Street Years*, was published in 1993. She died of a stroke at the age of 87.

Before the full force of Nazi persecution befell them, **ANNE FRANK** and her family moved from their home in Frankfurt, Germany, to Amsterdam in the Netherlands, where her father, **Otto Frank**, established a food products business. After sixteen-year-old **Margot Frank** was summoned for deportation in July 1942, the Franks went into hiding in a **secret annex** on the second floor of an Amsterdam commercial building. They were joined by Frank's business associate, **Hermann van Pels**, his wife Auguste, their fifteen-year-old son **Peter** (known in the published version of Anne's diary as the Van Daan family), and **Fritz Pfeiffer**, an elderly dentist (called Albert Dussel in the published diary). Sustained by Dutch friends who supplied food and other essentials, the group succeeded in eluding detection for twenty-five months by remaining silent and still during the day and moving about only at night after workers downstairs had gone home. It was in this claustrophobic environment that Anne Frank's extraordinary chronicle of adolescence took shape.

Shortly before their strenuous predicament began, Anne had received a diary for her thirteenth birthday on June 12, 1942. Addressing her diary as **"Dear Kitty,"** she recorded, with great wit and perception, the daily routine in the annex and her dreams for the future. The hopes of the group were greatly bolstered when they heard that the Allies had invaded France. Surely the war would soon be over!

The last entry in Anne's diary was August 1, 1944. Betrayed by a worker in the office below for the usual reward of five gulden ($1.40) per person, the eight Jews were arrested three days later. On the day that the Allies liberated Brussels, Belgium, they were among the last group of one thousand people to leave Holland. At the **Auschwitz** concentration camp in Poland, the men and women were separated. It was the last time Otto Frank—the only one of the group to survive—ever saw his family.

After the war ended in 1945, Frank returned to Amsterdam, where his Dutch protectors gave him Anne's diary, which they had found in the annex. In 1947, it was published as *Het Achterhuis* (The Secret Annex), and in 1952, it appeared in English as *Anne Frank: Diary of a Young Girl*. It was soon adapted into a play, which opened in New York on Broadway in 1955, and won a **Pulitzer Prize** for its authors.

Through interviews with forty-two people who had known Anne, **Ernst Schnabel**, author of *Anne Frank, A Portrait in Courage* (1958), learned that she had died of typhoid in the **Belsen concentration camp** shortly before it was liberated. "Her voice was preserved," Schnabel wrote, "Out of the millions that were silenced, this voice no louder than a child's whisper... It has outlasted the shouts of the murderers and has soared above the voices of time."

TONI MORRISON, whose visionary work about African Americans and the suffering of the human condition makes her one of the most significant writers of the twentieth century, received the **1993 Nobel Prize in Literature** for her book *Jazz*. Morrison was the first Black and only the eighth woman to win the prize since it was first awarded in 1901. Born in Lorraine, Ohio, as **Chloe Anthony Wofford**, her most vivid memories of her childhood included learning about Black folklore, music, myths, and storytelling, which was a major source of family entertainment. She graduated from Howard University in 1953 with a degree in English and changed her name to **Toni**. In 1955, she earned a master of arts degree from Cornell University and then taught at Texas Southern University. Two years later she returned to Howard and married architect **Harold Morrison**.

In 1965, Morrison became a textbook editor for Random House Publishing in Syracuse, New York, and later she moved to New York City as a senior editor in its trade department. While there, she continued her teaching career at State University of New York at Purchase (1969–1970), Yale University (1975–1977), and Bard College (1979–1980). Her first novel, *The Bluest Eye*, about a young girl's yearning for unattainable physical beauty, appeared in 1970. By the end of the decade, she had written *Sula* (1974), about the twenty-year friendship of two girls in the 1920s, and *Song of Solomon* (1977), for which she received the **National Book Critics Circle Award** and an appointment to the American Academy and Institute of Arts and Letters. The following year, **President Jimmy Carter (b. 1924)** appointed her to the **National Council of the Arts**. In 1984, she left publishing to become the humanities chair at the State University of New York at Albany, where she remained until accepting the Robert Goheen Professorship on the Council of the Humanities at Princeton University, becoming the first Black woman writer to hold a named chair at an Ivy League university.

Morrison received numerous honorary degrees, honors, and awards, including the Presidential Medal of Freedom in 2012, and her biography was featured in the PBS series *Writers in America*. Her other major works include *Tar Baby* (1981), which made her the first Black American woman to appear on the cover of *Newsweek* magazine; *Beloved* (1987), a moving account about the harsh legacy of slavery, for which she received the **Pulitzer Prize**; the play *Dreaming Emmet*; and a book of essays, *Playing in the Dark* (1992). She also authored several children's books, and even wrote the libretto for the opera *Margaret Garner*, which premiered in Detroit in 2005. Morrison said she was inspired by "things that had never been articulated, printed, or imagined...about Black girls, Black women. I don't want to redress wrongs. I want to alter the language and rid it of...its racism and fill the void with the voice of Black women. It is a risky business."

The first woman president of the Philippines, **MARIA CORAZON AQUINO** served a six-year term between 1986 and 1992. Assuming leadership of a country whose economic wealth had been depleted during the corrupt twenty-year dictatorship of **Ferdinand Marcos (1917–1989)**, she succeeded in establishing, preserving, and ultimately handing over a working democracy to a handpicked successor.

The daughter of a congressman and granddaughter of a senator, Aquino was born on her family's sugar plantation in Tarlac province. Receiving private Catholic school education in Philadelphia and New York, she set aside her law studies in 1956 when she married **Benigno Aquino Jr. (d. 1983)**, who later became leader of the opposition to the Marcos regime. In 1972, when Marcos declared martial law and arrested his adversaries, Benigno was imprisoned, and for the next seven years, Corazon acted as a liaison to his followers. In 1980, Benigno was released for heart surgery in the United States, after which the Aquinos and their five children lived near Boston for three years.

In August 1983, Benigno returned to Manila, where he was gunned down by government loyalists as he left his airplane. After twenty-six defendants were acquitted of his murder, Corazon became active with the opposition, traveling the country to rally people and to demand Marcos' resignation. Urged repeatedly to run for president, she agreed to do so in her husband's place when it became clear that she alone was popular enough to win. Using intimidation and sabotage, the 1986 election was rigged by Marcos supporters. However, a bloodless people's revolution led by Lieutenant General **Fidel Ramos (b. 1928)**, deputy chief of the armed forces, declared Corazon as president, and Marcos fled the country.

Sworn in as the seventh president of the Philippines on February 25, 1986, she immediately abolished the National Assembly and organized a commission to draft a new constitution modeled after that of the United States. She governed by decree and through local and national appointees until a new Congress was elected in 1987. Although she faced vast debts, political corruption, an ongoing guerrilla war between the army and Communist insurgents, attacks from Marcos supporters, and seven attempted coups by the military—the last of which in 1989 provided the final setback to the economic revival of the previous three years—Corazon's anointed successor, Fidel Ramos, became president after peaceful national elections in May 1992. Aquino accomplished what she had set out to do. She remained a notable political figure for the rest of her life and was involved in socioeconomic initiatives and charitable causes until her death in 2009.

Cosmonaut **VALENTINA TERESHKOVA** was born on a farm near the village of Maslennikovo, Russia. Her father, a tractor driver, was killed in **World War II**. After working in a tire factory, she joined her mother and sister to work in a cotton mill. She was an active member of the **Young Communist League**, and in 1959, she took up parachute jumping as a sport, at which she quickly became proficient. By the time she entered the space program, she had completed 126 jumps.

In 1961, inspired by the pioneering space flight of **Yuri Gagarin**, Tereshkova wrote the government to volunteer for the space program. After completing the rigorous physical and technical training on June 16, 1963, she became the first woman to be launched into space. Once aloft, she sent this transmission back to earth: "This is Seagull. I see the horizon. A light blue, a blue band. This is the earth. How beautiful it is. Everything goes fine."

In her craft, the *Vostok 6*, she completed forty-eight orbits over a period of three days, traveling a total of 1,225,000 miles. Soviet **President Nikita Khrushchev (1894–1971)** named her a **Hero of the Soviet Union** and awarded her the **Order of Lenin** and the **Gold Star Medal**. Taking the opportunity to chastise the West for their "bourgeois" attitude that women were the "weaker sex," Khrushchev pointed out that, on her historic flight, Tereshkova had remained in space longer than all four male American astronauts combined.

In 1963, Tereshkova married fellow cosmonaut **Andriyan Nikolayev** and they had a daughter, **Yelena**, in 1964. Her birth garnered great interest because she was the first child born to parents who had both been in space. Tereshkova continued her career as an aerospace engineer, traveling abroad to lecture about her experiences. In 1968, she directed the **Soviet Women's Committee**, and in 1987 she became head of the **Union of Soviet Societies for Friendship and Cultural Relations with Foreign Countries**.

◆ Founder of the **Children's Defense Fund (CDF)**, **MARIAN WRIGHT EDELMAN** is esteemed as the leading voice for children's rights in America. Born in Bennettsville, South Carolina, she was the daughter of a Baptist minister who expected his children to get an education and use it to serve their community. At Spelman College, she received stipends to study at the Sorbonne in Paris, at the University of Geneva in Switzerland, and in the Soviet Union. In 1960, she became active in the civil rights movement, participating in a mass sit-in at the Atlanta City Hall, where she and thirteen other students were arrested. This experience proved to be a turning point for Edelman, who abandoned a career in international relations to become a civil rights lawyer.

After graduating valedictorian in 1960, Edelman entered Yale University Law School. In 1963, she worked on a voter registration drive in Mississippi, and after graduation, she became one of the first two National Association for the Advancement of Colored People (NAACP) interns in Jackson, Mississippi. Between 1964 and 1968, while continuing her civil rights works in private practice, she headed the NAACP Legal Defense and Educational Fund. In 1968, she married **Peter Edelman**, a Harvard Law School graduate, and they had two sons. The couple were one of the first interracial couples to marry in the South, where such marriages had only just been made legal in 1967. Edelman realized that in order to effect systemic changes, she had to impact federal policy. Using a grant to study how to make laws work for the poor, she started the **Washington Research Project**. In 1971, she became director of the Harvard University Center for Law and Education. In 1973, she founded the CDF with the goal of securing long-term, fundamental services for children and making children's needs an urgent national priority. Edelman viewed CDF's mission as educating Americans about how to take preventative action in the areas of health, education, childcare, youth employment, child welfare, and family support services. In 1987, CDF was responsible for introducing the Act for Better Child Care. Its 1993 lobbying efforts centered on childcare and early childhood education.

Edelman served on numerous boards, including that of Spelman College, and commissions, such as the National Commission on the International Year of the Child in 1979. In honor of her lifelong work on behalf of children, she was given the Presidential Medal of Freedom in 2000, received over fifty honorary degrees, and was awarded numerous other accolades from organizations ranging from the National Women's Political Caucus, to Big Brothers Big Sisters of America and the 1988 Albert Schweitzer Prize for Humanitarianism. She wrote many articles, including "In Defense of Children's Rights" (1978), as well as several books, such as *Children Out of School in America* (1974) and *Families in Peril: An Agenda for Social Change* (1987), and *The State of America's Children* (2000).

A K'iche' Mayan Indian born in the remote northern highlands of Chimel, Guatemala, **RIGOBERTA MENCHÚ**, winner of the **1992 Nobel Peace Prize**, became one of the most powerful voices for the rights of indigenous peoples in the Americas. Growing up, she witnessed the brutality perpetrated by government forces on people—who make up more than forty percent of the country's population of nearly seventeen million. During Guatemala's civil war, the longest-running leftist rebellion in the history of the Americas, more than 100,000 people died in mass killings in the 1980s.

As a child, Menchú traveled with her father, activist **Vicente Menchú**, a founding member of the **Committee of Peasant Unity (CUC)**. In the 1983 book, *I, Rigoberta Menchú: An Indian Woman in Guatemala*, she described how her father was burned to death with other protesters when government security forces stormed the Spanish Embassy in Guatemala City, and how she and her mother watched in silence—so as not to be killed themselves—as soldiers tortured and immolated her sixteen-year-old brother and other so-called "subversives."

After her mother was murdered and her two sisters joined the guerrillas, Menchú went into exile in Mexico in 1981.

While in exile, Menchú continued to forcefully condemn the intolerable human rights conditions in her country, working with the CUC to focus world attention on the plight of indigenous peoples in Guatemala and elsewhere in the Americas, including the United States. She also was a vocal critic of American support of Guatemala's military regime, which in the early 1990s still averaged two "extrajudicial executions" or forced disappearances every day.

With the $1.2 million Nobel Peace Prize money, Menchú founded the **Vicente Menchú Foundation** to help Indigenous street children and the widows of murdered political prisoners and also to promote projects that preserve Mayan culture. While applauding the efforts of the **United Nations** to resettle refugees and help mediate Guatemala's civil war, she cautioned that, because the conflict in Guatemala was so longstanding and deeply rooted in the extreme polarization of rich and poor, it would take a long time to resolve.

For Menchú, the key issues in ending her country's strife were eliminating the oppression of Indians by Ladinos (persons of mixed blood), allowing indigenous people to maintain their culture, and creating a society based on mutual respect and equal participation. In 1996 she served as the presidential goodwill ambassador for the Peace Accords in Guatemala. After the civil war ended, she campaigned to have Guatemalan political and military members tried in Spanish courts for the torture and genocide they committed. Menchú ran for president of her country in 2007 and 2011. Although she did not win, her campaigns helped strengthen Winaq, the first K'iche'ean-led political party in Guatemala.

TRIVIA QUESTIONS AND PROJECT SUGGESTIONS

Test your knowledge with the following questions. The answers are on the pages listed.

1. At the first American women's rights convention in Seneca Falls, New York, in 1848, a document was introduced which made the first public demand for voting rights for women. Which two women organized the convention? What was the name of the document? Who wrote it? (See nos. 34 and 38)

2. What is "physiotherapy?" Who pioneered its use to treat polio patients? (See no. 72)

3. At dawn on the morning of August 24, 1572, the worst slaughter in the history of France began. It later came to be known as the Massacre of St. Bartholomew's Day and eventually claimed fifty thousand lives. Name the queen responsible and her reason for such a drastic measure. (See no. 18)

4. Who were the "Spartacists," and what did they oppose? (See no. 67)

5. Two popular English queens lent their names to historical eras. Who were they? (See nos. 19 and 44)

6. There are many women who are known by the "firsts" they achieved. Name the following trailblazers: a) the "first modern feminist," b) the "first woman mathematician," c) the "first woman doctor in Scotland." (See nos. 28, 10, and 54)

7. Who is considered to be the pioneer of smallpox inoculation in Europe? (See no. 22)

8. In the 1980s, the U.S. Department of Defense named its new systems implementation programming language after this early computer programming pioneer. What was the name of the program? For whom was it named? (See no. 39)

9. Twenty-nine of the women discussed in this book spent all or part of their careers in the teaching profession. Name at least 10. (See nos. 3, 4, 10, 23, 35, 36, 37, 41 45, 48, 49, 50, 52, 54, 62, 66, 67, 69, 73, 74, 76, 78, 80, 81, 83, 85, 93, and 96)

10. In conjunction with her husband, which woman scientist's work on the characteristics of heat and fire helped lay the foundation for modern chemistry? (See no. 27)

11. How much did Lewis and Clark pay the young Sacagawea for her services as a guide and interpreter on their 1804 expedition up the Missouri River? (See no. 33)

12. In the context of the American women's rights movement of the nineteenth century, what was a "Stoner?" (See no. 42)

13. Because of their courageous acts and exceptional bravery, these seven women came to be considered national heroines in their countries. Who were they? (See nos. 2, 8, 15, 32, 46, 53, 83)

14. Who was the first woman African American self-made millionaire, and what products did she market? (See no. 63)

15. Five women in this book had statues dedicated to their legacies—one by an

ardent admirer and four by the governments of their countries. Name the women and who was responsible for erecting their memorials. (See nos. 5, 7, 53, and 57)

16. What was the "Underground Railroad?" Who founded it? (See no. 47)

17. What causes the condition known as "phossy jaw?" What did this and other intolerable industrial working conditions lead to? (See no. 55)

18. What is the name of the oldest existing piece of Jewish literature? Who is said to be its author? (See no. 2)

19. Nobel Prizes have been awarded yearly since 1901 for merit in physics, chemistry, medicine and physiology, literature, and world peace. (Economics was added in 1969.) Name the women and years of the following awards: chemistry (See no. 62), literature (See nos. 78, 92, and 96), and peace (See nos. 48, 60, 88, 100). Which woman was the first to receive a Nobel Prize and the only one to receive two? (See no. 62)

20. What incident proved to be the catalyst for the American civil rights movement of the 1960s? (See no. 90)

21. Upon her death in 1872, what writer of scientific texts was acclaimed by the London Post as the "queen of nineteenth-century science?" (See no. 31)

22. In 1923, three years after the Nineteenth Amendment granted American women the vote, Carrie Chapman Catt wrote: "It is doubtful if any man...ever realized what the suffrage struggle came to mean to women... How much time and patience, work, energy, aspiration, faith, hope, and despair went into it. It leaves its mark on one, such a struggle." What was the first country to grant women the vote? What was the most recent? Are there still places in the world today where women either have limited access, or no access at all, to the right to vote?

23. Both Maria Montessori and Catharine Beecher were pioneers in the field of education. How do Montessori's learning methods differ from those used in traditional preschools or elementary schools? How many of Beecher's innovative ideas are in use today in modern classrooms?

INDEX

OUT NOW:

THE STORY OF
SIMONE
BILES

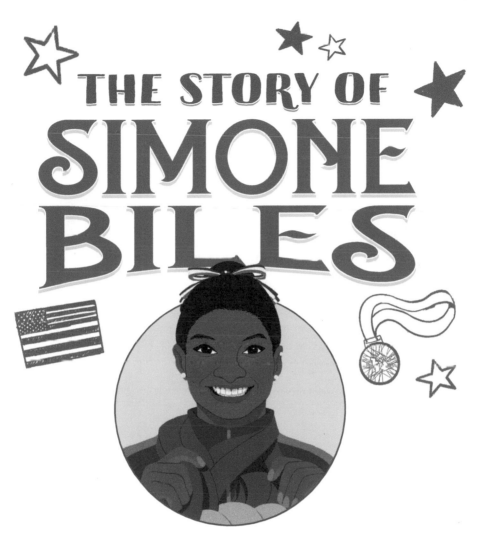

A Biography Book for New Readers

— Written by —
Rachelle Burk

—Illustrated by—
Steffi Walthall

ROCKRIDGE
PRESS

For Corrie—when you
put your mind to it, you
can do anything.

Series Designer: Angela Navarra
Interior and Cover Designer: Scott Petrower
Art Producer: Hannah Dickerson
Editor: Kristen Depken
Production Editor: Mia Moran

Illustrations © 2020 Steffi Walthall. Photography © PCN Photography/Alamy Stock Photo, pp. 48, 49; Leonard Zhukovsky/Shutterstock, p. 51. All maps used under license from Creative Market. Author photo courtesy of Alana Barouch. Illustrator photo courtesy of Clarence Goss.

Hardcover ISBN: 978-1-63878-841-6 | Paperback ISBN: 978-1-64739-775-3
eBook ISBN: 978-1-64739-462-2
R0